CHRIST IS THE MORNING STAR

When Celtic Spirituality Meets Benedictine Rule

EDITED BY
LINDA BURTON & ALEX WHITEHEAD

LINDISFARNE BOOKS

First published 1999 by
Lindisfarne Books
7/8 Lower Abbey Street
Dublin 1

Available in the UK from:
Veritas Company (UK) Ltd.
Lower Avenue
Leamington Spa
Warwickshire CV31 3NP

Lindisfarne is an imprint of Veritas Publications

ISBN 1 85390 482 1

British Library Cataloguing
in Publication Data.
A catalogue record for
this book is available
from the British Library.

Cover design by Colette Dower
Cover photography: Robert Cooper
Printed in the Republic of Ireland by Betaprint Ltd, Dublin

'The biggest challenge facing the Church of England today is not attendance or finance, but faith.'

Christopher Mayfield
Bishop of Manchester
Chairman of the Central Readers' Council
of the Church of England

CONTENTS

INTRODUCTION

This collection of essays, poems and prayers aims to enhance our appreciation of spirituality, so that our own lives will be enriched and so that we will be better placed to enable the spiritual growth of others.

The book grew out of a large national conference for Licensed Readers within the Church of England at the College of St Hild and St Bede at Durham University in the autumn of 1998.

In seeking a vision for Christian Ministry in the new millennium, we chose to revisit the spiritual roots of the English Church, which we believe come from both the Celtic and Benedictine traditions and which have a special relationship with the development of the story of Christianity in the North East.

We deliberately invited a mixture of nationally and locally known contributors, each with a significant vision of the value of our Celtic and Benedictine roots for the future of the Church. Many of them have a long-standing relationship with the Church in the North East.

Linda Burton and Alex Whitehead
Editors

PREFACE

The North East is proud, and rightly so, of its early saints, whose names, now household terms, grace countless schools and churches: Oswald and Aidan, Columba and Benedict Biscop, Herbert and Hilda, presently to be followed by Wilfrid and Chad. As their names tumble and cascade together in no special order, so they reflect the meeting of the cultures we are to explore in *Christ is the Morning Star*.

It was the year 597 when the meeting began, though Ninian of Whithorn might disagree. Pope Gregory had spoken his famous '*non Angli sed Angeli*', and sent Augustine (not of Hippo but of Canterbury) to become the Apostle of Kent, the first official Benedictine Mission to England, from whence Paulinus was to journey north to York. But the year 597 also saw the death of Columba of Iona, from whence Oswald was to summon Aidan, the first Bishop and Abbott of Lindisfarne and 'Apostle of England', who influenced Hilda by his gift of land and whose departing soul inspired Cuthbert to leave his shepherding and become a monk. But 597 was to be overtaken by 664 and the Synod of Whitby, with its subsequent and sorry parting of the ways.

1134 years later, today's Church is rediscovering its Celtic roots and, without losing its Benedictine Rule in the ordering of its liturgy, is learning to live with the untidiness of an unfinished world as well as celebrating the wonder of God's creative love; is learning to live with the chaos that erupts alike in soul and society as well as marvelling at the splendour of a North Sea gale; is learning to live with the confusions and contradictions of all God-talk as well as being silenced by the mystery of the eternal Trinity's encircling love.

There are in George McLeod's words, many 'thin places' in the north-east as well as Iona, where time and eternity inter-penetrate this world and the next. Whether Celtic or Benedictine by nature, we trust that you will find something that speaks to you of this glory in the grey.

Alan Smithson
Bishop of Jarrow

PART ONE
THE SHAPE OF WORSHIP

1

GETTING OFF TO A GOOD START

Linda Burton and *Alex Whitehead*

A Decent Cup of Coffee and a National Conference

In 1996 the editors found themselves sitting in a coffee bar in Coventry, hoping for a decent cup of coffee and looking for inspiration. They were part of a delegation from the Diocese of Durham to the Annual General Meeting of the Central Readers' Council held at Warwick University. If you are not an Anglican, you may be lost already. You, the innocent reader, may already be asking, 'What is a Reader and why the upper case "R"?' To experience the full flavour and purpose of this book you need an answer to this question.

In the Church of England, Readers are an order of lay ministers (they have sometimes been called 'Lay Readers', rather like the Methodist Lay Preachers). This order of ministry dates back to 1866, with its roots in the Office of Lector in the Post-Reformation Church. Readers are trained to preach, teach the Christian faith and assist in the leading of worship, while contributing to the pastoral ministry of the local Church. Bishop Alec Graham (formerly of Newcastle) liked to describe Readers as 'lay theologians', who would have the theological skills to reflect both upon the Gospel and upon any insights they may have into their daily lives and occupations. In this way, the Reader will bring a unique understanding of the secular world into the preaching and teaching ministry of the Church.

This establishes a powerful lay ministry alongside, and in partnership with, the ordained ministry, with a huge potential benefit to the work of the Church today. There are now over eight thousand Readers (and rising) in the Church of England alone.

The Bishop of Durham Looks to the Twenty-first Century

The Central Readers' Council is the national co-ordinating body for Reader Ministry, and the purpose of its 1996 AGM was to explore for Readers and the wider Church, the theme 'Vision 2000'. The keynote speech was given by Michael Turnbull, the Bishop of Durham, who described Reader ministry as 'an icon of neglected ministry in the Church down the centuries', that is, the neglected vocation both of the whole People of God and of specific lay ministries.

'I believe', the Bishop said, 'that today there is an urgency for deciphering the gifts that the Church has undoubtedly been given. We should be thinking of challenging and affirming people in their gifts, for they are there, surely, as a fulfilment of the promises of Christ to his Church. I believe that clericalisation of the Church has meant that so many gifts have been stifled. When people complain to me today that lay people do not respond to invitations to lay training, I perceive that to be a legacy of centuries when the Church has created a dependency amongst most of its members and an expectancy of too wide an array of gifts amongst a few whom we call clergy'.

Michael Turnbull sees that 'all ministry is derived from Christ and must reflect the internal and external dynamic of his relationship with the Father and the Spirit. The conclusion must be that ministry in isolation is untrue to God's own ministry in Christ. Partnership and sharing are keynotes of ministry. They must demonstrate God's ministry, supporting, caring, and complementing each other'.

The Bishop of Durham continues, 'As we move into the twenty-first century, this suggests that the development of shared ministry concepts needs to be accelerated. Clergy and Readers and, indeed, other ministries will seek to develop spiritual bonding which is derived from their oneness in Christ and their perception of the complementarity which exists in the Godhead. This is indeed a high doctrine of team ministry, but I do think that we need to aim for it, if ministries are to be valued and the work of sharing promoted'.

If the nature of ministry, as we move into the twenty-first century, is to be that of the whole people of God, much more characteristically 'lay' than 'clerical', and encouraged by a partnership of lay and ordained ministry, it must find itself looking outward into the world more than inward into the Church.

A Quiet Revolution

All of this is addressing a quiet revolution taking place in the Church of England and probably influencing the life of all of the long-standing denominations, Catholic and Protestant, in Britain and much of Western Europe. It is particularly significant in England, where the defining vision of the Church of England is based on being an Established Church. For a Church to be 'by law established' it must have a ministry to the whole nation: to every last city, town, village, person and blade of grass. At least in theory, nowhere in England is free from Anglican ministry, whether in the wildest, loneliest countryside, or on the bleakest urban housing estate. The whole country is divided into an unbroken network of dioceses and parishes. In return, every citizen has the right to expect ministry from a local parish church and to assume that it is available to them to interpret the great moments of life and death, through baptisms, weddings and funerals.

This blanket programme of ministry is supported by the fearsomely comprehensive Ordinal of the 1662 Book of Common Prayer. In the Ordering of Deacons, the Ordinal requires the deacon to 'search for the sick, poor and impotent people of the parish, to intimate their estates, names, and places where they dwell, unto the Curate'.

This is gentle pastoral ministry in comparison with the demands made by the Ordinal upon priests, who are to 'seek for Christ's sheep that are dispersed abroad, and for his children who are in the midst of this naughty world, that they may be saved through Christ for ever… and see that you never cease your labour, your care and diligence, until you have done all that lieth in you, and according to your bounden duty, to bring all such as are or shall be committed to your charge, unto that agreement in the faith and knowledge of God… that there be no place left among you, either for error in religion, or for viciousness in life'.

For the parish priest, the whole parish, for the bishop, the whole diocese, and for priest bishop and archbishop, the whole nation; such is the traditional vocation of the ministry of the Church of England. Even at the end of the second millennium of the Christian Era, Anglican bishops and synods (involving representative laity, clergy and bishops) have found themselves debating such national issues and taking a view on 'the bomb'; the miners' strike; the Falklands War; employment and unemployment; human sexuality; and commissioning such magisterial reports as *Faith in the City* and *Faith in the Countryside*, with high-quality analysis into prevailing social conditions.

The 1662 Prayer Book reminds the priest of 'how high a dignity and how weighty an office and charge [to which] you are called… and… how great a treasure is committed to your charge'. The priest is also reminded of the 'horrible punishment' that will ensue should anyone be hurt by his negligence. It is a wonder that anyone ever felt able to be ordained!

The aspiration to minister to everyone in a whole community as a parishioner, if not as an attending 'member', is a wonderful challenge, but one that the clergy are now incapable of meeting (as if they ever were). The numbers of clergy have radically diminished. For example, the Diocese of Durham has lost about a third of its paid posts in the last twenty years. Such changes in full-time ministry have been partly disguised by the practice of holding parishes in plurality and doubling up many posts that were once held separately. We continue to provide an appearance of the traditional structures, but without the traditional human resources. Consequently, there is the need for the quiet revolution already occurring in many places.

A new interest in Reader ministry is now evident, and Readers are in better heart than for some years past. Some dioceses and local congregations are experimenting with lay evangelists, lay pastoral assistants and other forms of unpaid lay ministry. Ordained ministers in secular employment and locally ordained 'voluntary' ministries are also being explored. 'Every member ministry' is being rediscovered, even in some of the far-flung outreaches of the Church of England.

A very English pragmatism, based on a more honest recognition of the Church of England's present straitened circumstances (involving reduced numbers of clergy, declining regular members and serious financial constraints), is now combining with a rediscovery of patterns of Church life as they emerged from the New Testament era. This involves the sharing of many gifts and graces within whole congregations. All this is already transforming the style of Anglican ministry as we approach the new millennium.

Yet revolutions, even of a quiet Anglican variety, may be hurtful, disruptive and rootless; thus stressing the need for good theology, a grounding in real spirituality and the participation in worship which possesses both life and depth.

It is evident that we cannot develop a realistic and hopeful Vision 2000 for an outward-looking collaborative and lay-focused ministry without it being rooted in a robust spirituality. Such a spirituality must be capable of providing the depth and inspiration without which all visions will flicker and fade.

A Cup of Coffee in Coventry?

The Durham delegation felt that we needed another conference to revisit our spiritual roots and that Durham would be just the place for it. Which brings us back to the editors in search of a decent cup of coffee and the inspiration to find the right formula for a conference, which would not only be helpful to Readers, but to any lay Christians.

Along with the coffee came the clue that any conference in

Durham would be shaped by Durham itself. Providentially, the title of the conference and the subtitle of this book were given by the location, for in Durham, and all that Durham stands for, Celtic spirituality really does meet Benedictine Rule.

What 'Durham' Means to Us

Nearly everywhere you go in Durham you are conscious of the majestic presence of the post-Conquest Cathedral, towering over the city from its almost island peninsula, encircled by the River Wear as it forms an 'oxbow' meander around the foot of the Cathedral hill. The conference was held in the College of St Hild and St Bede, and, as we listened to the lectures in the College's Caedmon Hall, we could not help looking through the large landscape windows to the Cathedral, as it watched over us.

Durham has always been a place of pilgrimage, based on the spiritual journeys, insights and life of prayer of the northern saints. Although dedicated to Christ and Blessed Mary the Virgin, Durham Cathedral was built as a shrine and final resting place for the body of St Cuthbert. Relics of the Northumbrian King Oswald were also buried in the Cuthbert Shrine behind the High Altar; while at the west end of the Cathedral in the Galilee Chapel is the tomb of the Venerable Bede, the monk of Jarrow and great historian of the conversion of England to Christianity.

We are taken by Bede into pre-conquest Northumbria, where Church and State were faced with the radical challenge of coming to terms with the competing and contrasting Celtic and Roman spiritual disciplines, who confronted each other at the Synod of Whitby in AD 664, hosted by St Hilda in the presence of the king, who would decide which discipline his kingdom was to follow. The creative tension of blending these two traditions into a spiritual and intellectual synthesis runs through much of Bede's *History of the English Church and People*. Bede himself was torn. He was not a neutral chronicler, being a monk of the Benedictine and Roman tradition, and yet he was an heir to the conversion of Northumbria by the great missionary saints of Lindisfarne, whose memory and example was a living inspiration to Bede and his contemporaries.

We maintain that Bede's great hero was Aidan, the founder of the mission to Northumbria, firstly from Iona and then from Lindisfarne. Bede's writing comes alive when he tells of Aidan. Yet, intellectually, Bede was convinced of the need for Roman order and Benedictine discipline. He had no doubt that the 'right' decision in favour of Rome had been made at Whitby. Nevertheless, a part of his heart remained with Aidan and his Celtic missionaries, while his head was with Wilfrid and Rome. We believe that this is why Cuthbert became so important to Bede. For, in so many ways, Cuthbert was like Aidan, with a similar spiritual motivation, the desire to pray and be close to God on a rocky island retreat, and yet also a powerful missionary, taking the Gospel through the wilds of Northumbria, with the gentle strength and personal holiness of Aidan. Cuthbert was the 'Roman Catholic' monk and bishop with the Celtic heart and lifestyle.

In recent years Celtic Christianity has become more widely rediscovered and immensely popular, being claimed by a variety of new developments and movements in Church life. Some of the most creative contemporary prayer writing has echoed and imitated the Celtic tradition; and the 'closeness to nature' of the Celtic communities has proved attractive to many Christians tempted by 'New Age' or stimulated by 'Creation' theology. Even the 'Church Growth Movement', for its part, has welcomed the example of the more adventurous missionary discipline of a 'church-planting' strategy, based on the minster sending out its missionary monks.

In the Celtic tradition the bishop is seen more as a spiritual and missionary leader, rather than a prince of the Church or the Church's chief executive. Here we seem to be presented with a more free-moving and free-flowing ecclesiology, with hermits or charismatic bishops, missionaries, and a seemingly more spontaneous and celebratory spirituality.

Yet Durham Cathedral very physically stands for the Bishop's Cathedral Church at the heart of a diocese, modelled on Theodore of Tarsus' system of dioceses and parishes. This presents a sense of order, clear authority structures and a more defined sense of corporate discipline. The prayer discipline of Durham Cathedral has always had a Benedictine base. Before the Reformation the monks kept the sevenfold Daily Office of Benedict ordered prayer, while after the Reformation, Dean, Chapter and choristers have maintained the morning and evening Daily Office of the Book of Common Prayer, celebrating the 'beauty of holiness' experienced in the restrained dignity of Prayer Book Anglicanism.

Based on a tradition of ordered communal prayer, which has extended from the Benedictine communities, through the 1662 Book of Common Prayer and the 1980 Alternative Service Book, we seek to value 'catholic order', with the Church of England having a national as well as local vocation to whole communities. However, we would also maintain that this obviously 'managed' form of Church Ministry needs the injection of the more charismatic, free-flowing spirit of our northern Celtic origins. The spirit of Iona and Lindisfarne has contrived to live on beyond the Synod of Whitby, even within the developing monastic communities of Jarrow, Wearmouth, Hartlepool, Whitby and Durham. A revisited Celtic spirituality potentially enlivens the Church beyond 2000. When Celtic Spirituality meets Benedictine Rule in a holy synthesis, we may discover a transforming spiritual energy which will enable a 'Vision 2000' to be realised in the English Church.

Reading Ahead

The following chapters are based on the lectures, workshops and worship of the Central Readers' Council Durham Conference. Throughout the chapters' essays, prayers, poems and songs, five themes will be woven:

- The meeting of the Celtic and Benedictine traditions
- Preaching
- Apocalyptic
- The Gospel, as a challenge for society and the world
- The People of God in the twenty-first century.

JESUS CALLS US

Jesus calls us here to meet him,
As through word and song and prayer
We affirm God's promised presence
Where his people live and care.
Praise the God who keeps his promise;
Praise the Son who calls us friends;
Praise the Spirit, who, among us,
To our hopes and fears attends.

Jesus calls us to confess him
Word of Life and Lord of All,
Sharer of our flesh and frailness,
Saving all who fail or fall.
Tell his holy human story;
Tell his tales that all may hear;
Tell the world that Christ in glory
Came to earth to meet us here.

Jesus calls us to each other;
Found in him are no divides.
Race and class and sex and language –
Such are barriers he derides.
Join the hand of friend and stranger;
Join the hands of age and youth;
Join the faithful and the doubter
In their common search for truth.

Jesus calls us to his table
Rooted firm in time and space,
Where the church in earth and heaven
Finds a common meeting place.
Share the bread and wine, his body;
Share the love of which we sing;
Share the feast for saints and sinners
Hosted by our Lord and King.

From 'Love from Below', *Wild Goose Songs,* vol. 3,
John Bell and Graham Maule.

CHRIST IS THE MORNING STAR

A Prayer of the Venerable Bede

Christ is the morning star
Who, when the night
Of this world is past
Brings to his saints
The promise
Of the light of life
And opens
Everlasting Day

To be found in the Galilee Chapel of Durham Cathedral near Bede's tomb.

PART TWO
WHEN CELTIC SPIRITUALITY MEETS BENEDICTINE RULE

2

WHERE CELTIC AND BENEDICTINE TRADITIONS MEET

Esther de Waal

To be in Durham provides us with an amazing situation in which to explore this subject, for we find ourselves in a holy place, with its ancient wellsprings of wisdom and tradition, where we can try to make a place of inspiration and of healing for ourselves, for our ministries, and for the future of the Church.

This question of the Benedictine and the Celtic traditions is a fascinating subject to explore, for it would seem at first glance so apparent that here we have two traditions that are extremely unalike. We have the Benedictine tradition, nurtured within the confines of the Roman Empire – even though it was in its demise, the great Roman concepts are still there: *gravitas, stabilitas, ordo* – while the Celtic flowers in those countries on the fringes of the Roman Empire, were essentially untouched by its cultural and social infrastructure. The Celtic world has saints, *peregrini,* who go wandering in coracles without oars, wherever the spirit will take them; it has monastic rules which vary from monastery to monastery, and are written in poetry; it is renowned for artistic achievements such as the Book of Kells or the Irish High Crosses, which are the expression of a unique, almost exploding imagination!

And yet both these traditions have, in my own personal experience of recent years, been extraordinarily significant in my life, and I guess that is true also of many other people like myself, lay Christians struggling to live out our commitment to our Christian faith and practice at the end of the twentieth century. In my own case I grew up in the Welsh Borders and as a result I knew something of local saints with names like Dubricius, but my father, who was a local antiquarian, gave me only the factual outline of their lives, and I had no sense that they were holy men and women whom I might come to know and revere. We would often go to tiny local churches associated with the saints, where so often there was a well, but that was simply because it was a nice place for a picnic. There was no sense that these could become places of pilgrimage, wells of living water, of healing. But I have been given a second chance, returning to live in a cottage in the same stretch of Border countryside, and now I see it all with open eyes, a changed perception. The kitchen window looks out across the fields to the Hill of the Seraphim; the local saints are men and women who tell me much about solitude and prayer and evangelism; those wells are now living and holy places for me.

There is something parallel in the way in which Benedictine monasticism came into my life, for at first I was blind and deaf to what surrounded me. I might have met St Benedict much earlier than I in fact did, for ironically enough my father was the vicar of a Shropshire parish, Bromfield, which had been a Benedictine priory, a dependant of the abbey of Shrewsbury (of Ellis Peters fame). The vicarage looked out over the ruins attached to the church and I knew all about the land grants and charters and boundaries, but it meant nothing at all. It was simply a pile of old stones, boring, dead, and totally irrelevant. The stones did not cry out, they were dead stones – they did not speak to me of a way of life, they did not influence my own Christian discipleship or enrich my way of praying. Then I was given a second chance, and when I spent ten years at Canterbury I found myself living in the prior's lodging of that great medieval monastic community, surrounded by magnificent reminders of that great monastic past, and then at last I came to discover the vision that had inspired the building of that place. And so, as a result, I came to read the text of the Rule of St Benedict and found that although written in the sixth century for men in rural Italy, it was neither remote nor inaccessible, but something immediately relevant to me in my daily life.

And so the story continues, for I now find myself living no more than four miles away from a Cistercian abbey – founded in April

1147, when St Bernard was still alive, by a group of twelve monks (always this same pattern based on the disciples) coming from France, settling down in this wild and remote part of the country, taming the land, and there creating a monastic community. But Dore Abbey is unique, for it alone amongst all the Cistercian abbeys in England has had a continuous life as a place of worship. At the time of the Reformation the property fell into the hands of the Lord Scudamore, a good friend of the Catholic-minded Archbishop William Laud, who reroofed the choir and reconsecrated the altar so that it became the local Anglican parish church.

The point that I am trying to make in starting in this personal way, is that when at last I began to see (to be aware of what was given, instead of being blind and unaware), it was through place: buildings, landscape, artifacts. It is this sense of being earthed in place, in the landscape, being rooted and grounded (sing both those words intentionally and with the full impact of the images that they carry) that I take as the first thread of this canvas which these two traditions give us. For both are deeply incarnational. Of course, everyone immediately associates Celtic spirituality with creation, with being close to the ground, bonded with the earth and with nature. This is the end of that disastrous split which has so damaged and twisted the way in which many of us first received our Christian faith, believing that it was really about being spiritual, going to church, saying prayers, being good. As a result we grew up finding a divorce between the material and the spiritual – something which George McLeod himself put his finger on so memorably on that day when I met him at Iona and walked round the cloisters with him, and he said, 'Everyone is saying what is the matter with the Church, the world today. The Matter is MATTER. The way in which we have spiritualised the faith, and set it apart from matter, whereas if we had remembered what the Celtic people always knew and still know, we should not be where we are today....'

But then this is also St Benedict's gift. I can still remember the delight and amazement when I read that small phrase in the Rule where he told me that I could handle the things of the kitchen or the pantry or the garden with as much reverence and respect as if they were the sacred vessels of the altar. Handling with reverence and respect essentially means recognising matter as God-given, seeing the tools of daily life, the times of the day, the light and dark, the stones and wood and glass of the monastery itself as things which can lead to God. Again what I read in the Rule was heightened by the actual experience of finding myself living in a Benedictine place. I discovered the system of underground tunnels which brought water to the monastery, a system of hydraulic engineering devised by an enterprising prior in the middle years of the twelfth century. The actual physical exercise of crawling through these most beautifully designed tunnels, the arches made of neat, square, cut stone, sensitively laid, in a place where by definition no human eye would normally see them, told me so much about the care that had gone into their construction. The lead pipes that carried the water from a small conduit on a low hill outside the city had been so wonderfully designed that today, seven hundred years later, water still flows through them, homage to their attention to the skills of mind and hand that they brought to bear here.

For this is holistic spirituality which recognises the importance of matter, of material things, of human physicality. But it is not 'creation-centred spirituality', a phrase that is now often popularly used to describe the Celtic tradition. This is grossly unfair and fails to do justice to the fullness of what the Celtic tradition brings to us today. It is of course creation-filled, that is undeniable; but the centre always remains the cross. It is symbolised in those magnificent High Crosses in Ireland, where in the centre of the circle (the cosmos, if you like, the Yes to creation) there is the figure of Christ on the cross. This is Christus Victor, who has overcome the forces of darkness and saved his people, and who holds out large hands, disproportionately large hands, to bless the world that he has both created and redeemed. Creation and redemption are held together; they are inseparable. So also in the Rule where we find that St Benedict gives a central place to the paschal mystery as the one essential on which the whole of life depends. In Canterbury Cathedral, in the Redemption window, which the monks placed at the furthest eastern point of the building, the portrayal of the crucifixion is its focal point. The inter-connectedness of cross and creation is the fullness of both the Celtic and Benedictine – and as so often, the Cistercian going back to the original impulse of the Rule brings this out so well, and not least in some of the twelfth-century writing on the crucifixion, which parallels that which is to be found in the Celtic. Is anything more moving than the words of Blathmac, as he stands in front of the cross, describing how the whole universe is suffering with the death of Christ?

> The sun concealed its proper light; it lamented its lord. A swift cloud went across the blue sky; the great stormy sea roared.

> The whole world became dark, great trembling came on the earth, at the death of noble Jesus great rocks burst open.

> A fierce steam of blood boiled until the bark of every tree was red; there was blood throughout the world in the tops of every great wood.

> The body of Christ exposed to the spear-thrust demanded harsh lamentation – that they should have mourned more grievously the Man by whom they were created.

The Cistercians bring an original, delicate sense of the image of the tree of the cross to their writing, as this from John of Forde in which the cross made of wood becomes the tree that is fruitful, and the apple tree is especially fruitful, so that we now sit in the shadow of the apple tree.

After we had lain so long in the shadow of death,
God's Son came, pitying those who lay in darkness.
He made us lie down
under the shadow of another apple tree,
and by that shadow
as much as by its fruits
he raised us to life again.
He came that we may have life
and have it more abundantly.

The movement from darkness to light was, after all, lived out daily in the monastic horarium. The day begins in the dark as the community would come down the night stairs, before dawn, for the first of the seven daily offices, Vigils, the word telling us of their intention – to be vigilant, awake, alert, attentive, waiting for the coming of the sun, for the coming of Christ. The Celtic year begins on 1 November, the feast of Samhain, as the earth moves into darkness, sleep, when the herds will be brought down from the summer pastures, and those that cannot be kept through the long winter months are slaughtered and their carcasses burnt in bonfires. And then the year moves towards its other axis, 1 May, Bealtaine, the celebration of the coming of light and life, when the flocks are taken back again to their summer pastures. It is interesting to notice incidentally that St Benedict also made 1 November the day for the change in the liturgical calendar, evidence, if it were needed, that the monastic life takes the changing seasons into account.

This movement from darkness to light is the movement from death to life, from Lent to Easter. The whole Benedictine journey is pointed towards Easter. And it is most important to remember that the Christ on a Celtic Cross is not the suffering Christ so often portrayed in the Middle Ages, a figure of which, perhaps, we are accustomed to think, but rather the warrior hero, who has many of the characteristics of the old pre-Christian Celtic beliefs, the hero who has saved his people from the forces of darkness, the Christus

Victor whom I mentioned a moment ago. But then on a number of crosses the crucified Christ is wearing the long white robe of the resurrected Christ – so that death and life, Good Friday and Easter, are brought together at the heart of the cross, in a symbolic statement which touches the heart, addresses the imagination in ways that words alone never could.

It is the power of the Celtic *imagination*, religion expressed in art and poetry and storytelling and praying that is song and music, that is so very attractive to a Christianity that has become left-brain weary. Yet I sometimes feel that this is sometimes rather too easy to say, and that it can become just a little dangerous to emphasise this so definitely. It is certainly one of the more attractive clichés of the moment – 'the Celtic speaks to the heart', but it does less than justice to the fullness of a tradition that counted scholarship and sound learning amongst its priorities, and which produced one of the greatest systematic theologians in the period between Anselm and Aquinas, namely John Scotus Eriguena, the ninth-century Irishman who went to the Continent to teach at the court of Charles the Bald. But equally, if the Celtic tradition can speak in intellectual terms, then the Rule of St Benedict is addressed to the heart – indeed the return to the heart is one of its central themes, a motif woven into what St Benedict is giving his disciples, caught in such wonderful aphorisms as 'as you make progress the heart expands' or 'a heart overflowing with the desires of love'. St Benedict's use of image is subtle, essentially scriptural, and if we are to get the riches of his message it is something of which we should be aware. To give one example: 'Listen my son', addressing each one of us as the prodigal, is the way in which the Rule opens, and at once we are plunged into the fullness of that story. The prodigal who is lost, has strayed, he comes to himself, listens to the word of truth, turns and returns home – and that chance to come home is precisely what St Benedict is offering, through the tools of the three moments of that story, which are also in essence the three Benedictine vows: obedience, which is simply about listening to the voice of God, responding and saying Yes; *conversatio morum*, which means ultimately *metanoia*, turning and returning; and stability, from the Latin word *stare*, to stand, meaning staying still, firm, being rooted in one's self, being at home in all the many levels that that word can carry.

Here again as we see the way in which these two traditions meet, I think that they are bringing us something that I believe we need to regain. I am sure that there are far too many words issuing from the Church at the moment in terms of reports, vision statements and declarations, with banners that carry slogans and flags waving in support of issues. In this situation I feel that it becomes increasingly urgent that we return to addressing the heart, to the use of symbol and image, of poetry and art, but equally urgent that we make sure that we do it within a serious and respectable intellectual framework, so that it does not tumble over into something lacking clarity or substance.

The sense of unity and diversity together is very much the Celtic way, and it is not something that is always recognised. For they all looked to Rome, revered Rome, saw it as a holy place which they visited, for it housed the tomb of St Peter. St Columbanus summed it up in a reproach to a bishop in Gaul when he said, 'Let Gaul, I pray, contain us side by side as the Kingdom of Heaven shall contain', which I see as an expression of that openness with which I feel we should be looking at the future, whether it is in this country or in the worldwide Church and the world. For its diversity has always been one of the charms of the Celtic tradition, springing as it does from six highly individualistic countries on the furthest fringes of the then known world. But this is also true of the individual houses of the Benedictine order, where one at once discovers their diversity, each with their own particular character and charism, created by the place itself, the circumstances and history of the past, the pattern of leadership. Yet they are bound by ties which mean that they are all brothers or sisters, members of one great monastic family – and that of course explains why Benedictines, whether Anglican or

Catholic, find that they worship together, speak the same language, and are at home in one another's houses, even though they also would not want to deny their differences.

The Benedictine tradition knows about paradox, just as the Gospel does. That is one of the reasons why I am so grateful for the way in which St Benedict teaches me to live with tension, holding together two things that might seem contradictory. As this century comes to its end I think that this is a message that we need to hear most urgently, for we are realising that life does not add up, and that we are frequently being pulled in differing directions. Are we to be fragmented and distracted or shall we try to learn to live with differences and contradictions in a way that is creative? To face this honestly becomes one of the most urgent and essential lessons for us today and tomorrow if we are to survive as individuals, as a Church, as a nation. So from St Benedict we see that in any life there is this double role: rootedness and journeying. The vow of stability commits us to being rooted, if not in 'one good place' on the ground in the words of Thomas Merton, then in our own interior selves, not seeking to escape, not drawn by those dreams and fantasies which we know only too well can be so beguiling. Yet St Benedict, master of paradox, knows that we must also move forward, and the vow of *conversatio morum* is the commitment to continual and never-ending transformation, the change from the old into the new. When Merton was challenged by the Dalai Lama to say what was the essential of Christian monasticism, he replied in one word: *transformation,* the change and growth of the old person into the new. And we might add that that is also as true of the institution as it is of the person.

This sense of exploration, movement, opening out to the new, is also given us so very clearly in the example of the Celtic *peregrini,* whose *peregrinatio* can again be so much better captured in images rather than words: they get into their coracles, without oars, to go wherever the Spirit may take them – and the goal of that journey is to seek the place of their resurrection…. But they also, in spite of this wandering, know about stability. It is very costly for them to leave the place where they belong, a tearing apart both from human kin and also from the wild creatures, from the earth itself, with which they are so closely united. Yet they do never fall into the trap of becoming what St Benedict spoke of so vividly when he castigated the *gyrovag*, the endless seeker, looking for the new, for distraction, or, again to use a wonderful phrase of Merton, 'the aimless wandering of the unsatisfied romantic heart'. For the journey would not be possible unless they had first found Christ, and already carried him with them. This short quatrain catches this so simply:

> To go to Rome
> Is much trouble, little profit.
> The King whom thou seekest,
> Unless Thou bring him with thee, thou wilt not find.

Those coracles, which so easily capture the imagination, were, however, not a small cockle shell, floating on the ocean with one lonely, pioneering saint on board – they were small ships holding a number of men, so that these journeys were a corporate venture, in which one depended on one's fellow oarsmen. Monastic life is essentially life in community, and even on Skellig Michael, that furthermost island housing a monastic settlement in those small beehive huts which perched so precariously on that rocky pinnacle, apparently rising sheer out of the ocean, was a shared life, with three or four men to each stone hut. A Celtic monastery is in fact better thought of as a monastic city, modelled on the secular ruler's, as circle after circle extends outward. In the centre would be the shrine of the founding saint himself, and then come the monastics, and after that, the lay workers, artisans, the married with their families, the children, the babies born into the community, the animals and the birds. Here is an extended family, which has something in common of course with what we also find in the Benedictine and Cistercian life, since here also there would be many besides the monks themselves – the young children being taught, for example, because of the Benedictine system of child oblates in the early Middle Ages; the lay brothers who were so essential a part of the Cistercian communities; and towards the end of the Middle Ages the system of the corridians, by which people at the end of their lives would come to live in the monastic complex and spend their final years in a life of shared prayer. Living with other people, and sharing in the burdens and services that enable a community to earn its living, is a totally realistic and inescapable human experience of being interdependent and interconnected, in which we all share. The Rule is, in the last resort, a practical handbook for this demanding and inescapable task of living at close quarters with other people. Ultimately, the monastic life raises only one question for the monk or nun, as it does for any of us, and that is 'Am I daily growing into a more loving person?'

Living with others, being part of an extended family, this corporate sharing, only becomes possible if one has first learnt to live with oneself. This is a truism, but the monastic tradition has always shown its grasp of the human psyche, an understanding of how our humanity works best. So St Benedict laid the foundation of his life's work as the founding father of a family of brothers by those years spent alone in the cave at Subiaco, when he learnt to live with himself, holding himself still before the gaze of God, in total solitude and silence. This relationship between the solitary and the community is central to Celtic monasticism, which is not surprising when we remember the connection between the Egyptian desert tradition and Ireland. The desert is translated into the *disserth*, the desert not of sand but of the forest, rocky outcrops on cliffs or remote islands where it was possible to retire from the world for shorter or longer periods. The place of the hermit is captured in the amazing nature poetry that came out of the experience of these solitary men and women finding themselves, by the vocation of their dedicated lives, in places of unparalleled beauty, which they saw with eyes washed clear by contemplative prayer.

I have a bothy in a wood only my Lord knows it; as ash tree closes it on one side, and a hazel like a great tree by a wrath on the other.

Fair white birds come, herons, seagulls, the sea sings to them, no mournful music; brown grouse from the russet heather.

The sound of the wind against a branching wood, grey cloud, riverfalls, the cry of the swan, delightful music!

I am content with that which is given me by my gentle Christ.

In the Celtic tradition we never find this withdrawal from the world as being a thing in itself, but rather something that is woven into the pattern of the life of ministry, an essential element in any apostolic or evangelical life. A man or woman would be a hermit for a certain length of time, at a certain period in their life, or perhaps for certain periods of the year. This was a time for the refreshment and the renewing of their energies so that they would return to life in the community, or to the burdensome and unwelcome role of serving the Church as a bishop, strengthened by this time spent alone with God.

A return to the desert is symbolically the way in which the Cistercian Order was started on 21 March 1098 when a group of Benedictine monks left Molesmes and 'set out eagerly for a wilderness known as Citeaux, a locality in the diocese of Chalon where men rarely penetrated and none but wild things lived, so densely covered was it then with woodland and thorn bush... and there they began, after felling and clearing the close-growing thickets and bushes, to build a monastery...'. Just as the Celtic tradition looked back to its links with the Egyptian desert (with St Antony of Egypt and St Paul of Thebes represented time and again on the High Crosses), so did the Cistercians recognise the foundational part played by Cassian in their own tradition, and the Cistercian reform was simply the attempt to recover this original insight. André Louf speaks of the analogy between the monastery and the desert: 'It is in the desert that the soul most often receives its deepest inspiration. It was in the desert that God fashioned his people.... That is why the monastery is a kind of prophetic place, an anticipation of the world to come....'

It is noticeable how much closer times of solitude can bring one to other people. The experience of Merton is well known and through his writings we can watch how the years in the hermitage are the years which saw his ever-growing commitment to the issues of peace and war, racial discrimination and social justice. We find the same thing when we read *The Hermitage Journals* of John Howard Griffin, the journalist friend of Merton who was commissioned to write his biography, a married layman who went to live for certain periods of time in the hermitage after Merton's death, how he not only learnt much about himself there, but came to feel closer to his wife and children.

Monastic life, whether Benedictine, Celtic or Cistercian, is about the *opus Dei*, the work of God, the priority of prayer, the uniting of praying and living so that praying is like breathing, a totally natural part of one's life – so that one breathes in God. 'At the sound of the bell drop everything', St Benedict told his monks. The great bell-towers that one still sees today in the Irish landscape, with their four windows pointing to the four corners of the compass, give us the same message – a handbell rung from that height, when the community gathered to pray, would remind the people living in the countryside around of the dedication of the monastic vocation. I have always felt that when we discover the treasury of prayer that was handed down in the oral tradition, from generation to generation in Ireland and Scotland, we find in this household religion the same principle as that of monastic prayer now translated into a lay spirituality. This is praying from dawn to dusk – we find prayers for morning, washing, making the bed, lighting the fire, for nightfall and sleep; for daily work, milking, weaving, driving the flocks and herds; prayer from the start of the year to its end; prayers for the birth of a baby and blessings for the time of death.

Here we have perhaps the happiest example of how these two traditions fulfil and complement one another. For the idea of praying without ceasing might so easily hang in the air as some abstract ideal but here we find it translated into lives that are those of ordinary lay people, busy, humdrum, mundane lives, comparable to those that we are all living. The *Carmina Gadelica* and the *Religious Songs of Connaught* are a lay spirituality of a people who were naturally contemplative in the way in which they lived and worked, walking totally unselfconsciously with God throughout their lives. Here are prayers that are song, blessing, poetry, which are easy and natural expressions of a contemplative and incarnational way of living. They are also, perhaps most significantly, immediate, simple, specific. The day starts with washing the face, making the bed, lighting the fire; it then goes on to the daily work of earning one's living, and these people are not ashamed to mention the teats of the cow or the thrums and treddles of the loom, just as St Benedict mentions every down-to-earth aspect of life in the monastery. It ends, like compline to make the day complete, with night blessings which recall the grave as naturally and as easily as the monk is living in awareness of death and life as inseparably linked. Here is the Benedictine *ora et labora* reaching us by way of the Celtic monastic way of prayer translated into the prayers of ordinary lay people, who show us the tenacity of that life and its relevance to any of us today as we seek to find God in our daily lives.

As Anglicans, we should be proud of the openness and the generosity of a tradition which believes in the *via media*, not as some sort of compromise, taking an easy, middle-of-the-road stance, but as being open to divergent expressions of the truth. In a Church and world which seem to be becoming increasingly polarised I feel it is vital that we do not forget this. By letting two streams flow in, and by holding them together dynamically, we are making a statement about the vitality that comes from being open to different expressions of the truth. In 1997 we did not see the faith of St Augustine and of St Columba juxtaposed as rivals; in 1998 we do not see the Cistercian tradition as anything more than returning to the source of monastic life and deepening it. This is something I have myself become very aware of as I have lectured or given retreats on both of these traditions in many differing places over recent years, and to people coming from different denominations within the Church. Both the Benedictine and the Celtic come from the earliest years of Christendom, originating in the fifth and sixth centuries, so that in them we find a place that is shared, and universal, taking us back behind and beyond all the divides and divisions of Church politics and parties, of denominational differences and labels. They come from those years that pre-date the schism of 1098 when the West lost touch with the East. They come from those years before the growth of the universities and the growth of the rational and analytical approach of the twelfth century, which has given us another split, one with which we are still living, that between the intellect and the feelings, between mind and heart. Here, instead, we touch something that is early, universal – 'primal' is a word that I like because it touches not only something that is deep, primal in my own self, but also something that is common, shared, universal to all of humanity. Here is something that is healing for the future and prophetic for the future, not only for ourselves but for the Church which we serve and also I believe for those who remain on its margins. I would wish that we could give our double heritage the respect that is its due: which means seeing it as a living spring and source, ancient but always new, a spring of living water to which we turn because it is the water of new life.

NOTES

The early Celtic poetry quoted here comes from A. M. Allchin and Esther de Waal (eds), *Threshold of Light, Prayers & Praises from the Celtic Tradition* (DLT, 1986). The quotations from John of Forde and André Louf can to be found in *The Way of Simplicity*, The Cistercian Tradition (DLT, 1998).

For further background on the Benedictine tradition see *Seeking God, The Way of St Benedict* (Fount Harper/Collins, new edition, 1996) and *Living with Contradiction, an Introduction to Benedictine Spirituality* (new edition, Canterbury Press, 1997). On the Celtic Tradition see *The Celtic Way of Prayer, The Recovery of the Religious Imagination* (Hodder & Stoughton, 1996).

3

A RULE OF LIFE FOR TODAY

Alex Whitehead

Introduction

At the age of seventeen, as a working-class grammar school boy from Bishop, Auckland, I was sent by my vicar to a vocations conference for sixth formers at St John's College, York. I think the vicar had his own agendas for me, but I was willing to go anyway. The prevailing atmosphere at the conference was a curious combination of the last blast of self-confident 'Prayer Book Catholicism' and a hint of a more evangelical, muscular Christianity. I cannot remember there being any girls and the tutors were all men, including some granite-chinned public school masters, some youngish priests who gave the impression of knowing exactly what they believed, and, in the old sense, a charismatic Franciscan, who first introduced me to the possibility of Christian socialism. (At least I discovered something of lasting value.) Michael Ramsey, then Archbishop of York, gave us an inspiring lecture, and the basic assumption of the Conference seemed to be that 'vocation' really meant Holy Orders or something similar, like Christian School Mastering and a rugged discipleship laden with moral values. We young men would go on to University, and out into the world as the next generation of principled young men flying the flag of English Christianity in a suitably Anglican, slightly understated, but morally determined way.

Inevitably, as the conference progressed, we were encouraged toward moments of decision, not in the evangelical way of 'knowing Jesus as your personal Saviour', but toward a committed eucharistic life of Christian service. Each of us was assigned a personal tutor. His task was to enable us to formulate a Rule of Life.

When we had designed our personal Rule, we were to discuss it with the tutor. And we were all so eager to please! Those were the last innocent days, when young chaps rebelled in acceptable ways. The 'Sixties and Rock and Roll' was still to become a universal creed and lifestyle for the young. For many of us, 'red-brick university' was to be our first taste of co-education and a more personally seductive world.

Nevertheless, we were already learning the sins of spiritual competition by attempting to second-guess what our tutors expected from us. Fortunately, my tutor was wise enough to ask me to simplify a Rule which would have hardly endured a week and which was manifestly designed for failure. My first experience of a Rule of Life almost instantly betrayed me to the experience of failure and the emotions of guilt.

How the Church betrays the young! The healing experience of true contrition is betrayed by the recitation of a checklist of predictable sins, while the life-giving exploration of a Christian Rule is diminished by constructs of pious propositions and boxes in which to tick off minor moral attainments. Where is the adventure of faith and an experiment with hope? Simply reduced to small successes, numerous failures and the insinuation of guilt. Even more terrible, what happens to you if you 'succeed' in ticking all the boxes?

> God, I thank you that I am not like other men: robbers, evildoers, adulterers – or even like this tax collector. I fast twice a week and give a tenth of all I get. (Luke 18: 11-12)

Discipline and Delight

Too often in the Christian Era, the spirit and inspiration of holy discipline and the joy in keeping a Rule to the glory of God has been corrupted by the legalism of those who abide by lists, who turn the spirit into Law and reduce the keeping of a holy life to the drudgery of daily attainment and the self-righteousness of standing 'justified' before God.

Rule, even Law, does not have to be reduced to legalism. It may provide the framework in which true freedom and growth is nurtured.

The great Psalm 119 illuminates the way in which discipline and delight journey together in a wonderful adventure of faith. There is no escapism from the toughness of life, but a joyful discovery of God's truth within it.

6. I will praise you with sincerity of heart:
    As I learn your righteous judgments.

11. I have treasured your word in my heart:
    that I might not sin against you.

14. And I find more joy in the way of your commands:
    than in all manner of riches.

15. For my delight is wholly in your statutes:
    and I will not forget your word.

32. Let me run the way of your commandments:
    for which you will liberate my heart.

47. My delight shall be in your commandments:
    which I have greatly loved.

54. But your statutes have become my songs:
    in the house of my pilgrimage.

97. Lord how I love your law:
    it is my meditation all the day long.

103. How sweet are your words to my tongue:
    sweeter than honey to my mouth.

131. I open my mouth and draw in my breath:
     for I yearn for your commandments.

147. Before the morning light I rise and I call:
     for in your word is my hope.

164. Seven times a day I praise you:
     because of your righteous judgements. (ASB, 1980)

Essentially a Rule must be appropriate. It must inspire a journey of exploration, aided by perceptive guidelines, themselves applicable to and interpretative of the real life of each traveller.

A working mother, anywhere, is travelling from a very different place, and meeting a very different series of obstacles and opportunities from that of a cloistered monk. The monk will encounter parallel but different challenges and joys. Both may be journeying to the same goal, but they will do it in their own particular way. What may be appropriate to the latter should not set the pace or define the Rule for the former.

Or, even among the parish clergy, take the case of a married priest with a young family in a busy urban parish. What shape will the Daily Office take? How many have felt guilty, when helping with children's 'teatime' or 'bedtime', and Evensong remains unsaid? The misdirected Rule cruelly damages and rapidly becomes a stumbling-block to the discovery of the way of true holiness. Guilt turns the Rule from becoming an inspiring friend into an oppressive task-master.

Cranmer, in the Preface to the Book of Common Prayer, requires that all priests and deacons 'say daily the Morning and Evening Prayer either privately or openly, not being let by sickness, or some other urgent cause. And the Curate that ministereth in every Parish Church or Chapel, being at home and not being otherwise reasonably hindered, shall say the same in the Parish Church or Chapel where he ministereth, and shall cause a bell to be tolled there unto a convenient time before he begin, that the people may come to hear God's Word, and to pray with him!' (BCP, 1662).

Cranmer's admirable Rule for the clergy already contains sufficient flexibility and adaptability to become a basic principle, rather than an unbending prescription. The bell is not the only means of communication available to us, and groups may pray together at set times and in a variety of sympathetic ways in church or at home, using a range of patterns and liturgies appropriate to the group and the time, without betraying the principle of Common Prayer.

Nevertheless, we must not forget the perceptive Religious, whether Benedictine or Celtic, who may have become for us the pioneer of principles, both illuminating and adaptable for other superficially very different pilgrimages.

The Need for a Rule and the Gift of St Benedict

The need to design appropriate Rules of Life has probably never been more necessary for a Christian. We live in difficult and tense days, defined in so many lives in terms of personal stress; whether of 'success', the 'burnout' of the seventy-hour week, or the 'failure' of the slide into the unwanted 'underclass', or the quiet despair of the family man made redundant nearing middle age. There is the ubiquitous fear, common to manager and labourer, of unemployment. Many live in one place, work in another and play somewhere else. There is the stress of mortgages, teenage crime, marital breakdown, the legacy of the cynical hedonism and selfish materialism of the eighties and the superficial familiarity and firstname 'sincerity' of the huggy nineties. Underneath is the loneliness and fragility of so many lives and the suppressed fear of old age. An earlier generation feared the workhouse for both the rural and urban poor. Our generation casts a disconsolate eye toward the growth of the industry of private residential nursing 'homes', when with other elderly strangers we will be neatly arranged round the walls of a sitting-room while the television will be speaking to nobody in particular, but will never be switched off.

Yet one of the greatest and most enduring religious Rules was formulated at a time of rapid change, some considerable danger and huge insecurity. St Benedict discovered his vocation at a time of extremes in wealth and poverty, with many social dislocations and insecurities, as the Roman Empire drew to a close. Rome had already been sacked and many trembled for the future. For us, the Empire has long turned into a Commonwealth, which in turn has been overtaken by the European Union. The British Isles themselves are devolving into their constituent parts and old and petty nationalisms throughout Europe are finding new strength.

The old institutions of State, along with the Monarch, are now seriously questioned, and in many eyes discredited or dis-established. State, including Church, is obliged to change. Established and traditional Churches of all denominations are in radical decline, replaced by the pick-and-mix marketplace of fickle consumer choice. The Age of Deference is now at last over, but relatively few feel true freedom. There is great uncertainty in both public life and private relationships, while discoveries in medical science seem to be racing ahead of our moral and ethical competence.

Now is not the time for the Religious to flee to the hermitage or the desert, for the true wilderness is to be found in contemporary urban life. The Benedictine Rule did not prevent the collapse of the Roman Empire, neither will a modern Rule remove all uncertainties and dangers, but it will help provide a true compass, focus and purpose for our contemporary journey towards God without seeming to escape from or evade the challenges of life and society.

Traditionally, the Benedictine Rule has offered a pattern of community life under God, based on stability and obedience in an unstable and fragmenting world, and *conversatio morum*, the flexibility to change, through conversion of life, guided within the community, but having room for a personal journey into God.

When the Church is strong, with a high profile in society,

comfortable with the world and familiar with the powerful, then there must be those who find the call of God driving them out of society and the institutional Church to live a radically different and challenging vocation, which, in itself, will offer a real critical alternative to worldly and churchly norms. In the past we see Cistercians called to be radical Benedictines, when the monastic life was becoming too comfortable. Hermits have embraced the wilderness to test the boundaries of vocation for themselves and for the Church. But, when the institutional Church is hanging on by its fingertips, the radical vocation will need to be worked out in the city, the urban areas and at the heart of the Church.

A contemporary Rule will not seek out the desert beyond the walls of society, but will seek to explore holiness of life within. Such a Rule may be informed and strengthened by the Rule of St Benedict, or the directives of Thomas Cranmer, but it will be shaped appropriately for the contemporary secular Christian.

The Example of the Psalmist

The contemporary Rule will seek to hallow and challenge contemporary life from within. It will wrestle with daily life, the Bible and tradition and will seek the right voice for prayer and prophecy for today. It will be rewarded by revisiting the Psalms.

The prayers of the Psalmist, sometimes brutal, often beautiful, were contemporary with the needs of the Psalmist, able to express anger, love, hope, fear and a desire for revenge, as well as a thirsting after God. Foolishly, the ASB 1980 places the violent verses in brackets, so that the modern squeamish Anglican would not have the discomfort of uttering terrible thoughts. The modern Anglican is not capable of thinking disturbing and unworthy thoughts? Many contemporary Eucharistic Lectionaries simply use the Psalms as a happy treasure trove of beautiful thoughts, studiously ignoring the verses that turn rough. Yet, the Psalmist sets the profound and profane side by side.

Psalm 137 provides a striking example:

The Profound

1. By the waters of Babylon we sat down and wept:
   when we remembered Zion.

2. As for our harps we hung them up:
   upon the trees that are in that land.

3. For there those who led us away captive require of us
   a song:
   and those who had despoiled us demanded mirth
   saying:
   'Sing us one of the songs of Zion'.

4. How can we sing the Lord's song in a strange land?

But by verse 7 we are approaching the Profane, from which the ASB 1980 seeks to protect us with brackets:

7. Remember O Lord against the Edomites the day of
   Jerusalem:
   how they said 'Down with it down with it raise it to
   its foundations'.

8. O daughter of Babylon you that lay waste:
   happy shall he be who serves you as you have served
   us.

9. Happy shall he be who takes your little ones:
   and dashes them against the stones.

This Psalm prayer, however violently disgraceful, is an honest unburdening and a wrestling with life and the agony of the innermost feelings. The join between the best and worst of our human feelings and thoughts are there for all to see. Healing may now have the opportunity to follow anger, after such a catharsis of expressing pent-up and destructive emotions.

Being True to our Daily Experiences

A modern Rule must be true to our daily experiences, allowing space for tirades of anger as well as the probing of beauty and peace. The troubled outburst as well as the spontaneous hymn of praise must be allowed expression and thus be turned into prayer, purified and sublimated by grace.

All responsible Rules must be based on daily prayer. Prayer does not need to be long or wordy, but it must be permitted to intrude upon our business and be subversive of our secular daily assumptions. The example of the monastic Rule and that of the Book of Common Prayer encourages our daily prayer to be in touch with the prayer of the whole Church. Not that we must all say the same prayer at the same time in the same way, but that we must be able to tune into a universal rhythm of prayer, which is part of the breathing, living Body of Christ. We may adapt, but would be foolish to abandon the basic principles of the Common Prayer of God's universal people praying across the centuries, in many languages and in every continent.

Our Rule of prayer will note the passing of the seasons, will rehearse and remember the central stories of the Bible and will hear the music of familiar bedrock phrases, as in the best of the Collects. The sheer earthiness of the Psalms comes highly recommended, but we need to understand how they can help unlock our own innermost struggles.

And there will be space for reflection, not too many words, but a patient waiting on God, allowing God to speak to us in his voice of perfect stillness.

Perhaps through keeping a prayer journal or leaving space for our own extempore intercession or prayer of adoration, we may discover how to extend our own vocabulary of prayer and reflect on our own journey through prayer.

In forming our basic prayer Rule we will give much thought to when we will make space for our daily 'Office'. There may be one longer time each week with a much shorter daily 'top up'. The Sunday Liturgy itself should be designed to send us out into the world with Prayer, Bible, Canticle and Song ringing in our ears.

We will be wise if we do not try to 'go it alone'. Even for the hermit, prayer is not a solitary occupation, for we commune with God in Trinity and we have the Word on our hearts. There are many ways of doing it, but we may choose to pray from time to time with others, outside the Sunday Liturgy. We may want to find a 'soul friend', a wise companion on our journey, or seek an experienced spiritual guide to help us reflect on the journey and find the appropriate way for us.

Daily life itself must be visited by the Rule and hallowed by prayer. The computer and the office telephone, like the little hills and the young lambs, are not beyond God's range and our prayer. If, for the monk, the work in the monastery field, kitchen and scriptorium were to be just as much a part of prayer, and the work of God, as the hours of prayers in the community chapel, then the commuters' train and the shoppers' supermarket trolley provide a forum for working out the Rule in the hallowing of time and space.

The Benedictine Rule assumes *conversatio morum*, the sharpening of the vows of obedience and stability in terms of moral conduct and behaviour, a movement of daily conversion to holiness of life. For the monk, this lifestyle will be shaped by the pattern of life in the monastery.

However, for the secular Christian, whether lay or ordained, *conversatio morum* will be developed in the context of the workplace, the home and the choice of leisure activity. This conversion of life will be in dialogue with our lives' context, but it will also be influenced by the movement of conversion within the local Christian community and Church. The whole Christian community should be a place of movement and a journeying into God and a reaching to the world. The Christian community, as well as the individual Christian, will be developing an attitude within the world by the degree to which the Church consciously or unconsciously stands over against or conforms to worldly values. It, and we, cannot remain untouched or neutral.

Revisiting Columba and Aidan

Revisiting the Celtic saint, Columba of Iona, Ian Bradley poses the question, 'On what journeys are Christians being led 1400 years after Columba's death? (Ian Bradley, *Columba, Pilgrim and Penitent*, Wild Goose Publications, 1997). Bradley is inspired and guided by Columba's characteristic ecclesiology and spirituality, which he defines as 'provisionality, pilgrimage and penitence' (p. 107).

If we seek to adapt Columba's ecclesiology in our own Rule-making, then provisionality will help us to define the Church and its life 'less in terms of its buildings and more in terms of its people, its ideas and its actions' (Bradley). The followers of Columba travelled light, were not overburdened with an over-provision of Grade I Listed Buildings and they took much of what they needed to be 'Church' with them. Their monastery bases were simple, of wood and wattle. The Psalm and the prayer of the community were in the mind and heart, the psalms recited on the journey. A contemporary Rule must be useful for a pilgrim, a walking, 'living stone'. It will enable you to be a bearer of the Spirit of the living God, your body becoming a living Temple of the Spirit.

Yet there is a need for place and space as part of the rhythm of life and prayer. The justification for maintaining so many ancient and Victorian large church buildings is that they are a 'sermon in stone', a reminder of God in the community and a place of sanctuary, as well as a springboard for pilgrimage. While not denying the truth in this, we are left with the question of why so many of these 'sermons' and sanctuaries remain mostly locked and are not accessible to the general public or even the faithful, except for the advertised times. They become a Gothic prison, locked and burglar-alarmed against the world, rather than a focus for prayer and a reservoir of the Spirit.

The sense of place may be provided by a church building, or even a particular chair in church. I like to find just the right place for my own 'daily office', with appropriate icons and my books at hand. It is good to have a place which is both comforting and familiar, but also numinous and awe-inspiring. It is helpful to find a place where there is a sense of Presence, where prayer has been prayed before, where you and others have discovered the intimate mystery of the presence of God. For me, I may look for my familiar seat in church or a particular Pastoral Centre in North Yorkshire. The place may be in the open air. My wife likes to return to a particular bench near a particular beach in South Wales, looking out to sea, close to where some of the old Welsh saints have walked. To find a particular place will help us to discover the presence of God in every place, thus hallowing the streets on which we pursue our daily lives. To retreat, and retreat is vital to the Christian journey, usually implies to return. For God is God both of the retreating and the returning, thus embracing the whole of life, rather than evading part of it.

Pilgrimage has rightly been seen as a journey to a place where God has been known, to a regularly recognised 'holy place'. Yet for Columba and his followers, the pilgrim's journey has often been to and through harsh and dangerous places. Pilgrim in *Pilgrim's Progress* had to journey through places of temptation or danger. Columba deliberately took on the worldly places to touch them with the living word and the martyrdom of 'witness'.

Columba was concerned to promote God-centred, righteous monarchy over the warlords and petty chieftains of his own age in order that social justice and righteousness transform the earthly kingdoms. He called the Church to be 'political and prophetic, not by making easy moralistic statements, but by costly engagement in the world' (Bradley, p. 111).

For many, the contemporary Rule will contain this element of world-embracing witness (true martyrdom) and prophecy. This is nothing less than holiness of life contributing to the conversion of society in terms of acts of service and the promotion of justice, integrity and peace.

'Provisionality' and 'pilgrimage' are complemented in Columba's ecclesiology and spirituality by 'penitence'. True repentance and 'a contrite heart' provide one of the most joyful experiences of Christian discipleship and the Rule must make provision for it. For Columba was a healer, and a contrite heart is one that seeks out healing, forgiveness and a growing purity. The Christian Community will engage in prayer and vigil for this world of fragmented societies, fragmented relationships, of warfare and civil war, and of easy gratifications at the expense of people and God-given ecology. Without true repentance there can be no true healing for society or for the individual.

At the heart of 'provisionality, pilgrimage and penitence' there will be a rhythm of prayer, rediscovering poetry and psalmody, song and symbol, leaving space for mystery and holiness, suspicious of the trite and 'matey', with an ability to know and respond to the world as the object of God's creative activity and spiritual outpouring. Then our lives, unselfconsciously, will become places where God is known, God has been, and God still visits.

We find one of the finest examples of the Columban way in Aidan of Lindisfarne, who was sent by the Iona Community to be Bishop to the Northumbrian Kingdom. His choice of Lindisfarne, an island joined to the mainland of Northumbria by a pilgrim's walkway at low tide, was to be the familiar place, the base community, reminiscent of Iona, from which the conversion of Northumbria would proceed. Aidan, when at home, could look across the bay to Bamburgh, where his beloved king had his 'palace'. The numinous Holy Island base had been established in order that Aidan and his monks could go out on missionary journeys, pilgrimages, and a claiming and naming of daily life and whole communities for God. Their mission was to transform society in a journey of discovery. God was not left behind them on Lindisfarne, but was to be known and rediscovered on the journey.

Their Rule was for the whole of life. Bede writes, 'The highest recommendation of his teaching to all was that he and his followers lived as they taught' (Bede's *History of the English Church and People*, Pelican Edition, p. 148).

Aidan was Bede's hero, despite the fact that he was of the Celtic rather than the Roman tradition. Bede's writings come especially alive when he discusses Aidan. For Aidan hallowed time and turned journeys into pilgrimages with the stones of the Bible and the rhythmic poetry of the Psalms. 'His life was in marked contrast to the apathy of our own times, for all who walked with him, whether monks or lay folk, were required to meditate, that is, either to read the scriptures or to learn the psalms' (Bede, p. 148).

Aidan had considerable influence over the king, through the king and upon the whole country. King Oswald was himself a remarkable man, who has also been commemorated as a saint. The partnership between bishop and king was to transform the Kingdom and change for ever the story of the North of England. Oswald extended the boundaries of Northumbria to include British, Pictish, Scottish and English subjects. 'Although he reached such a height of power, Oswald was always wonderfully humble, kindly and generous to the poor and strangers' (Bede, p. 149).

Even allowing a degree of hagiography and historical licence, the conversion of Northumbria was very different from Charlemagne's conversion of the 'Holy Roman Empire' at the point of the sword. Aidan and his monks had little alternative but to work with the king, but there seems to have been little sycophancy, and Aidan's combination of a gentle spirit, a tough body and a resolute mind seemed to penetrate the hearts of the people as well as of the king. Aidan would not 'offer' money to influential people, although he offered them food whenever he entertained them as host. But, if the wealthy ever gave him gifts of money, he either distributed it for the needs of the poor... or else used it to ransom any who had unjustly been sold as slaves. Many of those whom he had ransomed in this way later became his disciples (Bede, p. 149).

Aidan's mission was marked by a simplicity of life, a journeying from a community of prayer and discipleship set in a familiar but numinous place, with a rhythm of scripture, psalm and prayer to accompany the journey. It embraced the challenge of addressing both the king and public justice, as well as the conversion of a rough and wild people. It brought healing and holiness, combining provisionality with stability and an obedience to a Christ-like adventure of faith.

Bede writes that the first missionary sent from Iona to Northumbria was of 'a more austere disposition' and that he failed completely. The English 'refused to listen to him' and he reported to Iona that the Northumbrians were 'an ungovernable people of an obstinate and barbarous temperament' (Bede, p. 149). At the subsequent meeting of the Iona Chapter, Aidan replied, 'Brother, it seems to me that you were too severe on your ignorant hearers. You should have followed the preaching of the Apostles, and begun by giving them the milk of simpler teaching, and gradually nourished them with the word of God until they were capable of greater perfection and able to follow the loftier precepts of Christ'. The brethren soon realised that 'here was a fit person to be made bishop' (Bede, p. 149).

Conclusion

Those desiring a formula for constructing a Rule of Life, or a series of propositions toward a Rule, will be disappointed. I have no such Rule to share. We have visited Saints Benedict, Columba and Aidan; we have consulted Thomas Cranmer and lingered a moment with the Psalmist. I hope we have discovered that a Rule must be appropriate, flexible and contextual and that, although deeply personal, it will always remain public, breathing in the spirit of the whole body of Christ and living according to its rhythms.

Such a Rule, while addressing the inner heart and mind and known only to ourselves and God, will also look outward into the world in service, witness and prophecy. Paradoxically, our Rule will lead us on a journey seemingly travelling in two directions: deep into the heart of God and outward into the world. At its best, the Rule will enable us to discover that the God of the interior journey is the same God that we will encounter on our journey outward. The God of Bible, prayer and liturgy, the God of song and spiritual classic, the God of spiritual direction and the numinous places is also the God of the road and the city street; the God of work, home and leisure. I pray that we, reader and writer, may both find this Rule and, through it, the integrity of authentic pilgrimage.

4

PRAYER IN THE WHOLE OF LIFE

Angela Ashwin

'Read the Bible, pray every day, if you want to grow', says the old Sunday School song. But it's not as simple as that, is it? We fall into all sorts of pitfalls as we try to put this excellent advice into practice. One trap, which I call the 'God-in-a-box mentality', says, 'Prayer is the religious slot in my day, in a separate compartment from everything else; when I've finished praying I can get on with my life'. This kind of prayer can easily become a cosy escape from the realities of life. But there is another danger at the opposite end of the scale, which is equally misleading. I call this 'morning mist prayer', and it is found in remarks such as, 'Everything is prayer. Doing up my shoelaces is prayer. Playing tiddlywinks is prayer. You don't have to *think* about faith, or have special prayer-times, because it's all God's anyway'. This approach is so vague and nebulous that you quickly lose sight of it altogether. There is no substance or commitment here, and no sense of the power and presence of the God whom we encounter in prayer.

So wisdom and truth must lie between these two extremes. Yes, we do need spaces in which to give our total attention to God; times of quiet prayer renew and refresh us at the deepest possible level. And if we want to walk with God, and sing his song with our lives, we will need sometimes to stop and allow ourselves to do nothing else but come back into harmony with him. Yet, at the same time, all of life is the raw material for prayer. The more we ask God to show us how to 'pray without ceasing' as St Paul puts it (1 Thessalonians 5:16), the more God will make himself known to us in and through the fabric of our daily life, interweaving our hopes and desires and wills with the energy of his Spirit (like the interwoven designs on Celtic manuscripts).

One simple yet profound discovery can help us: *ordinary events of every day can become our Yes to God.* This may seem unrealistic when we are tired out and facing numerous pressures, constant demands and multiple irritations. How can you feel close to God when you have two telephones ringing simultaneously on the desk, or jam-covered toddlers clinging to your legs, or fume-filled traffic jams clogging your way to the office? It can help to look at these moments in a new way, seeing the interruptions and frustrations as the places where God is *closest* to us, in the thick of it all. I am reminded of Jesus being surrounded by jostling crowds on his way to see Jairus' daughter (Mark 5:21-43). What is so striking about that story is that Jesus stopped and gave the woman with a haemorrhage his full attention, in the middle of all that noise and movement. We may not always be aware of the fact, but Christ is present in the heart of our turbulence and chaos as much as in tranquil chapels and sunlit meadows.

We need to consider how much we are allowing the guilt factor to affect us. Sometimes guilt is a healthy thing: maybe I do need a pang of conscience, if I have allowed prayer to slip in my list of priorities. I call this 'green guilt', because, like good compost, it disintegrates, disappears, and leads to new life and growth.

But we may be carrying around a whole lot of unnecessary anxiety which becomes 'toxic guilt', *lodged* inside us, poisoning the system and discouraging us in our prayer. This may happen because we have latched on to a fixed idea of what we think our prayer Rule *ought* to be, and we try to impose it, willy-nilly, on our lifestyle. When it doesn't fit, we think it's our fault! Clearly we need to be liberated from such unrealistic expectations of ourselves, remembering that God is waiting for us to come to him *as we are, not as we think we ought to be.*

A good starting-point for prayer is to dare to *make into a gift to God* the very thing we feel is blocking or spoiling our prayer-life. It may be our lack of time, or even our lack of inclination to pray. When we do offer these things to God, we give him a chance to work in us, because we are opening up our situation to him. He doesn't wave a big stick at us, or tell us off for making such a motley offering. He comes to us *at our point of need*. So we needn't be afraid to make the mess and muddle of our everyday existence into the stuff of our prayer. Where else could we begin in any case?

Another useful exercise is to listen to our rhythms. Look at the overall pattern of your life, with its various ingredients, and ask God to show you how he is calling you to pray *within* your particular lifestyle. You may be like Margaret, a farmer's widow, who prays morning and evening as her sons go out for milking-time. Or you may be more like Jon, who works for a computer company and travels frequently all over the world. For him Morning and Evening Prayer are a non-starter, as he is often coping with jet lag, and has no idea what 'time' it is. So he has found a different rhythm, praying in the car (as many people do), meditating on the Bible at the start of every plane journey, attending a Saturday morning prayer breakfast, and going to a remote monastery every year for three days' solitude and silence. Most of us have a lifestyle that falls somewhere between these two, and we, too, can ask for guidance as to how God is offering us his gift of prayer within our own circumstances. It is a matter of going with the flow of our daily life, rather than trying to fight against the tide.

God is always present to us, and we can be aware of his presence at any moment. A 'thread-word' can help us to remember this; it is a short phrase or word that we take with us through the day; it can be a verse from Scripture, or any prayer or sentence that resonates with us. We can come back to it at any moment.

Another challenge is to discover our symbols. These usually come alive for us when we are living fully in the present moment, rather than being preoccupied with yesterday's troubles or tomorrow's plans. We need to *be where our body is!* Then we are more likely to be awake and alert enough to sense the touch of God through the things around us. Here are just a few examples:

An office worker walked past a certain tree every day on the way to work. He saw it but had never really looked at it. One day, in autumn, he suddenly found himself overwhelmed by the blaze of golds and reds and yellows in front of him. He stopped and gazed, and was late for work – but it didn't matter. The tree spoke to him of death and resurrection, and of hope in a world of pain and darkness. From that moment the tree became a vital symbol for him, and he found himself drawn back to a Christian faith that he had abandoned years earlier.

Or, there is the dinner lady who told me that she prays for each child as she puts their food on the plates. Or the High Court judge who prays every time he puts on his wig and gown that God will clothe him in the wisdom he needs for the huge responsibilities he carries.

A tree; sausages on a school plate; a judge's wig. What is your symbol? Maybe several things have been important to you at different times. It is good to go back to these from time to time, because they keep us rooted in what matters at the deepest part of ourselves; they keep us anchored in God.

Symbols cannot be forced. It's no good scouring the shelves of the pantry trying to squeeze a spiritual meaning out of every tin of pilchards or tube of toothpaste. On the contrary, we are letting ourselves go into the present moment, and being as open and receptive as we can to whatever God wants to give us.

Finally, there is a silence beneath all the sounds within us, deeper than the chatter inside our head. We can learn to dip into that quiet place at any time, in the 'inner room' of our heart (Matthew 6:6) where God is waiting to meet us. On a practical level, we can take a tip from the Old Testament. The Israelites were often rebuked for being a 'stiff-necked people' (cf. Exodus 33:5). We can learn from that, and become 'free-necked people'. Try it! Release the tension in the muscles in your neck, and, as you do so, ask God to open you up to the free flowing of his Holy Spirit. Use a 'thread-word', and let it lead you from your head to your heart, into your still centre with God. You can do this at any moment.

Whenever we pray, in whichever of the countless ways that are open to us, we become a little less fragmented, and find ourselves drawn together by the loving magnetism of the God who is always calling us to himself – and then we discover that he is the God who gives himself away.

O GOD, YOU SEARCH ME

O God, you search me and you know me.
All my thoughts lie open to your gaze.
When I walk or lie down you are before me;
Ever the maker and keeper of my days.

You know my resting and my rising.
You discern my purpose from afar,
And with love everlasting you besiege me:
In every moment of life or death you are.

Before a word is on my tongue, Lord,
You have known its meaning through and through.
You are with me beyond my understanding:
God of my present, my past and future, too.

Although your Spirit is upon me,
Still I search for shelter from your light.
There is nowhere on earth I can escape you:
Even the darkness is radiant in your sight.

For you created me and shaped me,
Gave me life within my mother's womb.
For the wonder of whom I am I praise you:
Safe in your hands, all creation is made new.

Based on Psalm 139, by Bernadette Farrell
(OCP Publications, 1992: 5536 NE Hassalo, Portland OR, 97213)

TAKE, O TAKE ME AS I AM

Take, O take me as I am;
Summon out what I shall be;
Set your seal upon my heart
And live in me.

(WGRG Iona Community,
Glasgow G51 3UU, 1998)

A PRAYER FROM THE PROSLOGION

Anselm, Archbishop of Canterbury

My God
I pray that I may so know you and love you
that I may rejoice in you.
And if I may not do so fully in this life,
let me go steadily on
to the day when I come to that fullness.
Let the knowledge of you increase in me here,
and there let it come to its fullness.
Let your love grow in me here,
and there let it be fulfilled,
so that here my joy may be in a great hope,
and there in full reality.

Lord,
You have commanded, or rather advised us,
to ask by your Son,
and you have promised that we shall receive,
'that our joy may be full'.
That which you counsel
through our 'wonderful counsellor'
is what I am asking for, Lord.
Let me receive
that which you promised through your truth,
'that my joy may be full'.

God of truth,
I ask that I may receive
so that my joy may be full.
Meanwhile, let my mind meditate on it,
let my tongue speak of it,
let my heart love it,
let my mouth preach it,
let my soul hunger for it,
my flesh thirst for it,
and my whole being desire it,
until I enter into the joy of my Lord,
who is God, One and Triune, blessed for ever. Amen.

PART THREE
MAKING THE SPIRITUAL JOURNEY

5

CUTHBERT AS MODEL PREACHER

David Day

Readers in the Church of England do a lot of preaching. And they do so in a context where the sermon is viewed with amused bewilderment, if not with hostility. There is a widespread popular assumption that sermons will be monumentally boring. William O'Malley advised preachers to 'presume they would rather feed their children to crocodiles than listen to you'.

Therefore, it may seem strange that I should want to look at St Cuthbert as a model preacher, with any idea that this exercise might be useful for us. There is a great chasm between Cuthbert's world and our post-modern age. Contrast the excitement when Cuthbert came to preach. 'Now it was the custom at that time amongst the English people, when a clerk or a priest came to a village, for all to gather together at his command to hear the word, gladly listening to what was said, and more gladly following up by their deeds what they could hear and understand.'[2] We would like to say, 'Well, no change there, then!' In practice, we often find ourselves preaching in churches where we feel there is more life under the flagstones than in the pews.

I grant the problem. I grant also that we may be dismayed by the way Bede and the anonymous author of the Life of Cuthbert handle their subject. They concentrate on the miraculous; we suspect that they are less picky about the facts than we would like; they certainly idealise the saint and they place over his deeds and character an overlay of scripture which invites the reader to see Moses or Christ recycled in him. Add to this the burden of holy history. Comparisons with saints always make me feel inadequate and there are many occasions when I could cheerfully strangle Cuthbert. These considerations raise difficult questions for us in our post-Enlightenment fastidiousness and scepticism about heroes. Yet we know we dare not lose our critical faculties.

Nevertheless, I do not want to lose the idea of the model or paradigm either. Thomas Heffernan's book, *Sacred Biography*, shows that writing about saints operates on different principles from those applied to modern history writing.[3] It is based on *instructio*, that is, the need to instruct the reader. It represents personality 'as a type of transparent membrane through which the author is intent to show the continual passage of God's grace'.[4] 'Sacred biographers saw little that need be contradictory between the worlds of fact and fantasy; both fact and fantasy were signs to the acute observer of the nature of things, different signs to be sure, but none the less signs revelatory of truth'.[5] I love the comment of one medieval biographer who said 'it is difficult, *though not impossible*, to write the life of a saint about whom one knows absolutely nothing'! The story's value resides in its capacity to reveal a 'taken-for-granted world'.

As to method, I have extracted the references to Cuthbert as preacher in Bede's Life of the saint and the anonymous Life and propose to engage in a conversation with this material. The portrait of Cuthbert, the preacher, has immense power to surprise us, precisely because the world it takes for granted is not our world. It can challenge presuppositions; provoke analogies with our time; move us by speaking of one who was a brother in Christ and a human being just as we are; inspire us (this is the power of the holy history or the myth); and stimulate fresh understandings, insights, reconceptions and reconstructions of our situation. So, for good or ill, let us begin.

1. To Penetrate Those Parts That Were Far Away: The Preacher's Strategy

Many experts on Celtic Christianity have written about *peregrinatio*. I can't say much that's new. It is wandering – literally going out and coming back. The geography of Lindisfarne makes going and coming an obvious strategy – back to the security of the island for worship and community, then out at low tide for mission and service. Of course, there is nothing especially Christian about wandering about. One source says: 'The demons put the spirit of restlessness into a man.' Moreover, *peregrinatio* may not seem to suit the Anglican parochial system or the general philosophy of 'let nothing be done for the first time'. We like the line in the hymn that says, 'for nothing changes here'. So what is the special element which turns curiosity or nosiness into a Christian virtue?

The wandering needs to be at the impulse of the Spirit of God. The theology of *peregrinatio* is that of God the Holy Spirit driving the Church outward to Judaea, Samaria and the uttermost parts of the earth. God calls Abraham to wander about, dropping altars where he stops and then move on. The idea of the pilgrim people comes from the theology of 'here we have no continuing city', though Steven Travis has described the Church as the best disguised set of pilgrims you could ever find.

I have tried to find the equivalent of *peregrinatio* for Anglican Readers. We are not particularly mobile. Doing a turn for a neighbouring Church isn't quite the same thing. What is its essence? And will it translate as a metaphor, even if not literally?

I suggest that it is about restlessness, unfinished business, responding to a divine discontent. It describes a willingness to encounter God, in David Jenkins' term, as 'the great disturber' and to respond to him with openness and a desire to change. I know this is a tall order. Woody Allen said, 'If you want to make God laugh, tell him your plans.' He always seems to have something else in mind and it's a good job he doesn't show us his plans in advance for many of us would have heart attacks. But if we are open to divine discontent, then how might it show itself?

i) *Peregrinatio*, for the preacher, might mean not getting into a rut. It might mean refusing to be satisfied with one's present state as a preacher; being prepared to continue to read; to work at the craft; to go on courses; to try things out. And in particular perhaps, *peregrinatio* might show itself in a willingness to experiment with my style of preaching and to find a friend who will speak honestly to me (though probably not my wife or husband). It will mean working at the voice, the mannerisms, the clichés, my standard form, whether three points and a poem or not. Certainly there is a need for experimentation with form. Since the Bible uses dozens of ways of communicating, why should we be reduced to a method that is sermonic and immediately recognisable as such? At a service in Durham Cathedral I heard a sermon on Church unity in the form of a parody of A. A. Milne's 'The King told the Queen and the Queen told the dairy maid, "I would like a little bit of butter on my bread".' Why can't that count as a sermon? When was the last time you heard a sermon as a piece of satire? Yet the form was fine for Isaiah. We need to be open to new methods of communicating.

ii) *Peregrinatio* might show itself in a deeper way. One of the exciting results of missiological research has been the rediscovery of the *Missio Dei*, the mission of God. Mission is not bringing God to people, bridging a gap between the life of heaven and a lost world. Putting it this way sounds as if God wasn't doing much until we arrived. *Missio Dei* declares that God is already at work and has got there long before us. We are not doing things to people and hoping God will catch up. We are being called to join God in his work which is already going on. *We* are the ones who have to catch up. What does that mean for the preacher? Perhaps, that as I sit down to prepare, I should remind myself that God is already saying lots of things to this congregation. My job is to discern what that word is and speak my words in the context of his words. This shifts the emphasis in preparation, and certainly, it removes entirely the idea of the sermon as homework, drudgery, a burden.
W E. Sangster said, 'As you climb the pulpit you should be saying, 'let me get at them'.

iii) A third way in which *peregrinatio* might show itself is in a deep desire to seek and to save the lost, a deep desire for evangelism, accompanied by a bias towards the outsider. We must always be asking the question, 'What will this sound like to those outside the holy club?' Sometimes this will mean physically going where they are – preaching in public houses, clubs and other unusual venues. During missions, I've spoken in gyms, at afternoon flower-arranging classes, at make-up and hair-styling evenings and men's breakfasts. But more than this, it will also entail a disciplined attempt to understand where people are. That will mean listening to them and letting them set the agenda. It may mean watching unsuitable programmes on TV. I'm glad I watch *Friends, Spin City* and *Frasier*. I force myself to watch *The Big Breakfast* and not only in Lent. We will work hard then, on analogies and illustrations drawn from their world. This will affect our vocabulary as well. There is an emptying called for from us. For example, I am not interested in sci-fi or aliens, but a colleague of mine is, and has written apologetic books to pick up what is a major interest for thousands of people. I am not engaged by the 'Diana factor', but the rest of the world is. Twenty-three million people watched the England-Argentina game during the World Cup. Twenty-six million watched the shoot out. I'm not sure we should get ourselves into the situation of having to ask, 'Who is David Beckham?'

It was said of Cuthbert that, 'To each one he gave varied advice with exhortation suitable to his character; that is to say he always knew beforehand what advice to give to any one and when and how it should be given'.[6] Cuthbert's desire that each should hear the Word in a form customised to the individual, is paralleled by recent work on respecting the hearers and listening to the congregation and those who are not in the faith. Work done by Mark Greene, John McClure and Roger van Ham explores this theme.[7] These writers press the question: 'What will this sound like to those outside?' We forget how remote our preaching can be – remote to the new Christian who read in her Bible, 'Put to death the old man' and yet quite likened her husband to the man who asked Bill Hybels (founder of Willow Creek and seeker-sensitive services), 'What are those numbers you keep saying?' (They were biblical references.)

As we take account of our listeners, we show forth the folly of God's love for people, the lunatic economics of the shepherd who leaves ninety-nine to find one lost. Here, we reflect God's commitment to his people, the fact that he is already in mission. Cuthbert's schedule is impressive. 'Now he was wont to penetrate those parts especially, and to preach in those villages that were far away on steep and rugged mountains, which others dreaded to visit and whose poverty as well as ignorance prevented teachers from approaching them…. He would often not return for a whole week, sometimes two or three weeks, and occasionally, for a full month, summoning the rustics to heavenly things by the words of his preaching.'[8] His priorities are clearly with those who have not heard the good news.

2. Nor Did Their Hope Deceive Them: The Preacher's Power

The really irritating thing about Cuthbert is that his preaching is never without effect. His sermons *do* something: they nourish and build up those who hear them; when he speaks, things happen. The issue for us is the value of preaching – what are sermons for?

For example, when Cuthbert teaches, his work is often followed by baptising those who listened.[9] 'Greatly improved and strengthened by his teaching they go home rejoicing…. They don't arrive at home for Sunday lunch saying, "what on earth was he on about this morning?" His conversation was seasoned with salt; consoled the sad; instructed the ignorant; appeased the angry, for he persuaded them to put nothing before the love of Christ.'[10] His preaching corrected errors. For some profaned the faith or, forgetting the sacred mystery, wandered from the truth. Cuthbert was concerned to convert them from a life of foolish habits to love of heavenly joys. At Medilwong he preaches and then says gently, 'Is there anyone in the village still suffering from the pestilence so that I may go forth and preach to him and bless him'.[12] And he goes and restores a child. The most dramatic account of the effect of Cuthbert's preaching is in Bede 22, a summary statement: 'Now many came to the man of God, not only from the neighbourhood of Lindisfarne, but also from the remoter parts of Britain, having been attracted by the report of his miracles. Such people declared to him either the sins they had committed or the temptations to which they were exposed, or revealed the common troubles of mankind by which they were afflicted, hoping that they would get consolation from a man of such sanctity. *Nor did their hope deceive them.*'

Most of us would settle for such an assessment of our preaching. Is there anything to learn from it or are we content to relegate the account to the kind of starstruck, hero-worshipping that affects people who are fans of holy people? Is it just hagiography at its most typical?

What intrigues me is the taken-for-granted assumption that something would happen when Cuthbert preached. Sermons are expected to do something. They are not a boring monologue. Suddenly I encounter a man who expected things to happen in a culture where people expected the preached word to affect their lives. He and they were serious about preaching, they gave a high value to the preaching of the Word.

How might this affect me?

i) This kind of account forces us to ask of our preaching, 'What is it intended to do?' And, 'How am I going to get it to do it?' That is, it compels us to ask questions of aim and construction. We have to face the question of the *point* of the sermon. It might also force me to ask about the intended *effect* of this sermon. What am I hoping will happen? What will it do for people? Often we rehearse some Christian insight and leave it there. 'So, this Lent let us all go with Jesus into the wilderness.' (Hmm. Good. Fine. But what does it mean?) I don't want to compare preaching to selling second-hand cars, but the car salesman is not content with a few remarks about cars. He works to a forty-eight-point system with a definite end in view. Moreover, this concern with ends might also lead me to check with members of the congregation the effect the sermon has had on them in reality. What did they recall? How did it intersect with their lives? What questions did it leave them with? What disappeared from their consciousness?

ii) The assumption that sermons do something might lead us to a serious attempt to re-educate the congregation. A student of mine went to Africa on placement. She wrote back, 'At last I believe in preaching.' She had been sceptical about the value of the sermon and then entered a culture where people hung on the words, listening to the Word. Is it possible to revive a culture which assumes, 'God could speak to me today. God will speak to me today, if I listen carefully enough?' Have you noticed how congregations behave differently at conferences and at parish weekends? There is a much higher level of expectation. It may be possible for us to reinstate the sermon, in our own minds and in the minds of those who listen, as a proper vehicle for the word of God.

iii) Perhaps we might also remind ourselves of the things that sermons are quite good at. We are told often enough that people don't remember them, that they've forgotten your main points by the time they've got home, that sermons are a bad teaching tool, that in a media-saturated culture most people's concentration span has shrunk to that of a lobotomised gnat and so on.... But sermons *are* good for some things.

Sometimes, for example, a preacher will articulate what people are feeling but aren't yet able to verbalise. She will put into words an idea or a feeling which 'I didn't know I felt until she said it'. Another preacher will interpret raw experience, helping people to see their stories as part of the Christian story, a process which we might call 'refraining' or 'look at it this way'. Often the sermon will do no more, though importantly, than rehearse old truths, the necessary task of 'worldview maintenance'. We need more to be reminded of old truths, than be taught new ones. For example, I recently heard a sermon on the *Friend at Midnight*, and was struck by how powerful the images of God as friend and father were when one turned to prayer. Often we do not so much need tips on praying, as we do assurance that the God to whom we pray is a friend. 'Here I

am, it's midnight and I am faced with an emergency and have no
resources to help this person who has come to me in great distress.
The God to whom I turn is a friend at midnight, not grumpy or
curmudgeonly, needing to be shamed or nagged into a response. He
is a friend. So pray on, however stupid it seems.' Here, no new
sermon is needed but rather, a rehearsal of old truths so that they
may be heard anew in my present situation. Sermons perform many
roles. At the right moment they will comfort and console, exhort
and strengthen, correct and admonish, instruct and teach or offer
vision and hope. Through a sermon, people may catch a glimpse of
that other world and may see something of the glory of God. Walter
Brueggemann states confidently, 'People change by the offer of new
models, images and pictures of how the pieces of life fit together –
models, images and pictures that characteristically have the
particularity of narrative to carry them. Transformation is the slow,
steady process of inviting each other into a counter-story about
God, world, neighbour and self. This slow, steady process has as its
counterpoint, the subversive process of unlearning and disengaging
from a story we no longer find to be credible or adequate.'[13] In this
slow, steady process the sermon plays a vital role.

iv) For Cuthbert, the sermon was never free-floating and
detached from the rest of his ministry or the ordinary lives people
were leading. His sermons were always part of a package. They
were, as far as we can tell, never a disembodied or isolated word, a
set piece of oratory, a rhetorical *tour de force*. They were a part, in
other words, of the whole ministry of the man and his sending
community to the whole person of his hearers. They were often
accompanied by works of power or works of mercy and compassion
(I love the combination of 'That I may preach and bless'). Thus, a
sermon is not an essay or something culled from a book. It is woven
into a movement of God's grace.

This implies that the best preaching is linked into the whole
ministry of the Church: its healing services; prayer groups; liturgy;
music; house groups; visiting strategy; baptism; and bereavement

visiting. The sermon ought not be an add-on, something an individual undertakes in isolation from the rest of the Church. Happy is the Reader who is incorporated into the ministry of the clergy, who has input at a worship committee, who knows the part he or she is to play in the planning of the whole series of sermons, who will find the content of the sermon taken up in discussion groups later in the week. We hear a lot about singing from the same hymn sheet, but preaching can still be a lonely business and often unnecessarily so. Yet there is no more fulfilling experience than to preach to a congregation which in some sense 'owns' your sermon. I have no idea whether you, like Cuthbert, will raise the dead after next Sunday's sermon but your preaching ministry ought to be part of the whole ministry of the people of God. Cuthbert's preaching was woven into his life; it could not be detached from his teaching, his caring, his community or his miracles. If preaching is no more than saying a few well-chosen words, then we should not be surprised if it sounds like an interlude within the main business.

3. A Window Of God's Grace: The Preacher's Personality

In a much-quoted saying, Phillips Brooks observed that 'preaching is truth mediated through personality'. It couldn't really be otherwise, could it? The issue, however, is one of how that truth is mediated and how much personality ought or ought not to show. Man can be a window through God's grace. Should the observer's eye ever rest on the glass or always look through? Is the glass stained-glass? How much does the message depend on the person?

The assumptions made in Bede and the anonymous *Life* are that message and person are one. The lives assume an integrity in the preacher. God speaks through the words of a particular person. In an extraordinary way, he honours the preacher's personality and experience.

i) The implication of this assumption is that God has things to say through you that can only be said by you. They require your: personality; gift with words; experience; good and bad bits; sense of humour; face; hands; capacity to do impressions; and appalling laugh. This is a great encouragement, I think, because it is an encouragement to be oneself in the pulpit. One does not need to attempt to be someone else, although all too often the effect of the great preacher is easily recognised in his or her disciples. Recent writing on the women in the pulpit suggests that what we understand by preaching is changing as more women preach. I mistrust stereotypes but it has been said, for example, that women handle scripture differently, explore feelings more sensitively and so on. I would not be surprised if that were so and, if it were, that it would be of a piece with the God who loves to incarnate his message in human beings.

ii) The second way in which the personality of the preacher is linked to the message is in Cuthbert's holiness of life. Our sources take it for granted that the light of God shone through his person and that the message was carried by that holiness of life. This is why the works follow the words. In Cuthbert, the curtain between heaven and earth is paper-thin. This is why he possesses the gift of discernment; he can see that other world. He can also see the hearts of people, as Jesus could. He has stood in the council of the Lord, like the prophets of old, and so is able to see when a fire is a false fire devised by Satan to distract people from the word. How nice it would be if we had such contact with heavenly realities, that we were able to discern distractions, fads, passing fashions and nine-day wonders as false fires. If only we were such people that could discern the hearts of men and women and hear their unspoken cries and pains. In a moving passage 'a religious man, specially dear to the man of God' finds his wife much vexed by a devil. He sends a message to Cuthbert that his wife is sick almost to death but does not reveal that she was 'afflicted with madness for he was ashamed to declare that a woman once so religious was oppressed by a devil'. Cuthbert goes with him and the man spends the journey weeping because of the degradation of his wife. Cuthbert, of course, knows what is really wrong and begins to console him.[14]

Now, though these stories strike us as quaint, they continue a biblical tradition which assumes that if you walk with God, something of that companionship will rub off. Illustrating this theme, Killinger writes on the importance of silence in the preacher's life. This is the source of the numinous power attaching to the person who has been with God. It results in the shining face of Moses as he comes down from the mountain. Killinger asserts, 'There is no preaching without presence, no speaking without listening, no talking without silence'.[15] Silence discovers reality, shapes character and bestows form and meaning upon language. Killinger speaks of a crisis of language in our world. The preacher can all too easily become like Lucky in *Waiting for Godot*, who spouts incoherent but impressive-sounding philosophical babble whenever a hat is placed on his head. 'Cliché is the opposite of silence. It is language from which all silence has been removed'. He writes of a Brother Antoninus, 'The man's words still bore the husks of silence upon them'. The invitation to those of us who prattle like Lucky is to spend precious moments every day in listening to God, to read the poets, to take vacations from speaking, 'if the malady of speech is too much upon us'. We are not surprised to read of the brightness of the light of Cuthbert's angelic countenance.[16]

iii) A third way in which Cuthbert's personality affected his preaching was in his style and manner. 'His conversation was seasoned with salt', 'His discourse was pure and frank, full of gravity and probity, full of sweetness and grace...'.[17] The biographers assume that who you are will affect the way you speak. This does not mean that we shall all preach with ponderous good taste but that our words will reflect not only our personalities but also some facet of the character of the Christ in whose name we speak. One implication of this is that preaching must take account of pulpit ethics. The gentleness of our tone ought to be genuine and not a false wheedling designed to manipulate the hearers. Similarly, I doubt if we will rant or preach angry sermons, working out our own hang-ups, prejudices and resentments in the name of the Lord. We will be careful about plagiarism in the pulpit. A friend of mine was writing a book on illustrations and was worried to find the same illustration circulating round a particular Christian constituency but claimed by different people, all of whom were confidently declaring that the experience was something which had happened to them personally. Again, it is easy to use other people's experiences without their permission. Even when confidentiality is preserved, there is an element of violation in this practice.[18]

iv) Linked with the genuineness of the preacher is his or her vulnerability. There is something profoundly moving about Bede's description of Cuthbert at Mass.[19] 'He was so full of penitence, so aflame with heavenly yearnings, that when celebrating Mass he could never finish the service without shedding tears.' And when hearing confessions: 'Sometimes when wrongdoers were confessing their sins to him, in his pity for their weakness he would be the first to burst into tears....' Cuthbert was a WYSIWYG saint. What you saw is what you got. He was not so buttoned up that no one could get past the carefully carapaced pulpit persona. Is this kind of openness embarrassing? Should the preacher hide decently behind the message? It is heartening to read that the preacher's woundedness may be one of the most significant resources that he or she can bring to the sermon. Hans van der Geest writes: 'I will awaken deep experiences in others to the extent that I am able to reach myself. (Otherwise) I am drawing from a well which is going dry.'[20] None of this is manufactured or false, however. It is but another example of how life and words should be in harmony.

4. Preaching The Word Of Life: The Preacher's Message

There is a fourth area where Bede's presentation of Cuthbert's preaching ministry may intersect with our concerns. We want to know, understandably, what Cuthbert said. What was the content of his sermons? Did he proclaim some special message guaranteed to unlock the hardest heart and cause even the rough North Easterners to fall down and confess their sins? If so, can we, in the style of those who go on courses to learn how to sell double glazing, re-use his material, latch on to his secret and so acquire a system that cannot fail, a go-anywhere message which will work in any time and any place?

The answer is certainly no. What does strike us, however, both in Bede and the anonymous Life, is the very high estimate of the content of what Cuthbert preached: word of God, word of life, word of the Lord, way of truth, way of life, way of salvation. For both authors Cuthbert is faithful to the word which brings people to God. We are not surprised to learn that he preaches 'after the manner of the apostles'. He is faithful to the tradition. The way the events in his life are assimilated to the scriptures (for instance, he brings water from the rock like Moses) shows an overlay of scripture placed over him. It is scripture which provides Bede with his models. Cuthbert is faithful to scripture and to the tradition.

In the context of preaching, scripture, tradition and faithfulness are all worth thinking about. For Anglicans three concepts interact – scripture, tradition and reason. Scripture is the master tape but we recognise that the *interpretation* of scripture – what it meant, what it means and what it ought to mean for us – is a task which requires a community and that constitutes tradition. Texts do not interpret themselves. The third term, reason, recognises that the way we handle scripture depends partly on what we hear the voices of our culture saying to us. This is so because what is to count as being reasonable changes from generation to generation.

This means that the idea of faithfulness can never be set in concrete. Indeed if faithfulness just meant repeating without thought the teaching of the Bible then we would still be wearing tassels on our clothes. Faithfulness needs to be distinguished from being frozen in time; we are not talking about being a crustacean or a mollusc, expending a great deal of energy on not moving. Shibboleths often masquerade as faithfulness. You say exactly what the holy writings say and then you can't go wrong. Unfortunately, we all know that that is when an idea or a teaching which once had great power becomes just a catch-phrase, a cliché, or a way of disenfranchising groups that won't say precisely what we want them to say. Biblically, shibboleths are quick ways of discovering who the enemy are so that we may slaughter them.

On the other hand, faithfulness has got to mean *something*. It cannot mean being blown about by every wind of doctrine. If it did, then it would be difficult to see what we were being faithful to. You can restate, reconstruct and remythologise to the point that something vital gets lost. Those who entered the Promised Land redrew Yahweh in the style of Baal. This was so much more exciting. It involved infant sacrifice which solved the problem of All Age worship, and sacred prostitution which really brought in the outsiders. But the *Baalisation* of Yahweh was precisely the subject of Elijah's crusade. Something vital was being destroyed so that what was claimed to be faithfulness to a core idea was in fact infidelity and adultery. There is always an accompanying problem, of course: my baby is your bath water and my bath water is your baby. That is partly why there is disagreement about women's ordination and gay issues.

The Archbishop of Canterbury addressed this in his Presidential Address to the Lambeth Conference in 1998. Pointing to the Bible as the sovereign authority interpreted in the light of tradition and reason, he said:

> And of course that doesn't mean that we use words like tradition and reason as cop-outs to do whatever we want! What it does mean is that there is an interplay of Bible, tradition and reason which never undermines the primacy and authority of Scripture.[21]

i) I want to reiterate the Archbishop's stress on the primacy of scripture. Week by week we stand in the pulpit to speak the word of the Lord, the word of life, of truth, of salvation. That is a high and holy calling. It's a terrifying one as well. Scripture determines our message. Scripture gives us our authority. It will not do to paraphrase the headlines from the Sunday paper or inveigh against social evils which are far from our doorstep or attack views which nobody in the pews in front of us would dream of holding. In the Lives of Cuthbert the saint appears to let scripture frame his message. We should do no less. God still speaks through scripture when it is faithfully and prayerfully proclaimed. Letting the scriptures speak is still the prime task of the preacher. Unfortunately, the biblical passage has been captive to the lectionary for too long, so I am delighted to see that the new lectionary has delivered us from the tyranny of the *theme* where the main topic of interest was the dexterity of the preacher in juggling the three balls of Old Testament, Epistle and Gospel. In a theme-driven situation, the preacher needed to second-guess the mind, not of Christ, but of those who devised the lectionary, and was inclined to preach the theme by picking bits out of the three lections, whether they were part of the thought of the individual readings or not. Worse still, some preachers were reduced to rehashing the brilliant juggling acts of Joy Tetley or Tom Wright in *The Church Times*. Therefore, I approve of the revival of interest in expository preaching if that means letting the passage say what it wants to say and in the terms in which it says it. And I think there's a lot to be said for preaching the passage, the whole passage and nothing but the passage.

ii) The primacy of scripture shows itself in a second way. Even before Thomas Long's *Preaching the Literary Forms of the Bible* homileticians had been asking that preachers should take the way scripture communicates as seriously as what it has to say. For some time now those who write about preaching have been exhorting us to study the literary form of the passage. A psalm is not a proverb; a gospel is not a letter. A psalm of complaint is not the same thing as a hymn of praise. What the passage says is partly dependent on how it says it. So *the form* is important in understanding the passage and in catching its mood and tone. We can go further. The form of the biblical passage may well give us a pointer to the form of the sermon which results.

iii) Along with the new emphasis on form goes a renewed interest in rhetoric and the discovery that scriptural passages are not just about telling us things, giving lots of new information; they are also intended to do things to us. Like a good sermon, scripture is persuasive speech. It wants to change us – to inspire, correct, lead to repentance, force us to think harder, move us to tears or action, or nerve us for acts of courage or resistance. What does 'Blessed are the pure in heart' mean? And more importantly, *why* was it said? Is it meant to console me, annoy me, direct me? What happens when you declare a particular group of people to be blessed – especially if you are speaking with authority? Listening to scripture means letting scripture do things to me. This style of listening will not only mean that we take scripture seriously but that it will affect the content and direction of our sermons.[22] These are some of the ways in which the idea of the primacy of scripture cashes out in actual sermons.

iv) There is a fourth implication of the call to be faithful to scripture. As we respond we are compelled to admit that every generation has a tendency to try to keep scripture in a bag. We are no different and we are not going to let the Bible loose, if we can help it. Normally we don't do this deliberately but traditional interpretations have produced a canon within a canon and a set of meanings which are accepted without demur within the community of the faithful. Some examples may help to make this idea clear. We might ask when was the last time we heard a sermon on money which took the standard New Testament line. Money on the lips of Jesus is nearly always a snare and a delusion, unwelcome baggage on the way to the kingdom. Those who have money have a job getting through the needle's eye. Now most of the sermons I've heard on money concentrate on prosperity and giving generously to God's work. Seldom do they describe money as the

Mammon which one cannot serve if one is going to be faithful to God. Read commentaries on 1 Corinthians before the modern charismatic movement and you will wonder how commentators could have been so blind. However could they have missed all that discussion of speaking in tongues and spiritual gifts? It is one of the benefits of feminist readings of scripture that we can hear the Bible speak in a different tone and are directed to things that the Bible has been saying for years while we have been deaf to them. It was only when I read Phyllis Trible's *Texts of Terror* that I realised that, in the story of Hagar, God is the only character who has the decency to call the slave woman by her name. Again, when discussing stances in scripture, Craddock asks a probing question about where the preacher stands in the text.[23] For example, where are you in the story of the woman of the city? Next to Jesus, with the Pharisee, with the woman or a bystander? In the story of the labourers in the vineyard, are you the worker hired first who toiled all through the heat and burden of the day? Or are you the one no one would hire, the recipient of grace upon grace, none of it deserved? I remember preparing a sermon on Peter and John at the Gate Beautiful. The congregation and I were Peter and John, of course. The sermon was about our responsibility to those who sat, literally and otherwise, at our gate. Halfway through the preparation the thought struck me – on what grounds do you identify with Peter and John and not with the crippled man? The sermon set off in another direction. Craddock observes that the congregation is often left ruefully saying to itself, Today our minister is Jesus and we are the Pharisees – again!

All these examples make a similar point. With God's help we must try to listen again to the Bible, to let it speak to us in its own terms. It's been called 'looking for trouble', in other words, looking for that bit which shocks, surprises, scandalises, overturns our expectations, denies and criticises our taken-for-granted world. It may be there that God wishes to speak his new word. But, whatever the result, the attitude is all-important. We come to our preparation with a firm conviction about the primacy of scripture which translates into careful and disciplined reading in the confidence that the Lord has yet more light and truth to break forth out of his word.

In Cuthbert, despite the long passage of the years, we recognise someone who belongs to our time even as we belong to his. He is a brother in Christ. In his faithfulness I recognise the apostolic message, the gospel in which I stand. I hear a continuity with the past even while I understand that I will have to put the old wine into new skins. Were he with us, Cuthbert would be mystified by my references to the Spice Girls, to the Internet, to being cut up at a roundabout. Given that he knew nothing of football I don't know what he would make of the phrase 'He's got all the time in the world to pick his spot'. But then that's not just Cuthbert's problem.

Then I listen to him and discover that he is teaching the Celtic equivalent of an Alpha or an Emmaus course. He covers the key topics: the ministry of the law, the teaching of the faith, the virtue of temperance, the practice of righteousness. His sermons contain a substantial teaching content, for he is not ashamed of doctrine. In Cuthbert's mind there is truth to tell and something to be affirmed. This is so, he says, this is the way the universe is.

As I listen I hear him linking the word preached to the mundane world, making connections with ordinary life – the kindling of fire, the milking of cows. I see him using the experience of the eagle bringing food as a way into a sermon.

And then I hear him speak to ordinary people, and to me, that they should be devoted to our Lord and put nothing before the love of Christ. I hear him 'set forth plainly before their eyes the greatness of future benefits; the grace already bestowed, that God spared not his son but delivered him up for us all'. I hear him calling them 'to heavenly things by wholesome admonitions' and trying 'to turn people from a life of foolish habits to a love of heavenly joys'.[24] And as I listen, he moves me to turn again to my calling and my craft.

NOTES

1. Walter Burghardt, *Preaching: the Art and the Craft* (New Jersey: Paulist Press, 1987), p. 45.
2. Bede, *Life of St Cuthbert*, chapter 9.
Mark Greene, *The Three Eared Preacher* and 'Is anybody listening?' in *Anvil*, vol. 14, no. 4, 1997, pp. 283 ff.
3. Thomas Heffernan, *Sacred Biography* (New York/Oxford: OUP, 1988).
4. Ibid., p. 157.
5. Ibid., p. 71.
6. The anonymous *Life of St Cuthbert*, 4:1.
7. John McClure, *The Round Table* (Pulpit, Nashville: Abingdon, 1995).
Roger Van Harn, *Pew Rights*.
8. Bede, ibid.
9. Anonymous *Life*, 2:5; 2:6.
10. Anonymous *Life*, 3:7.
11. Bede's *Life*, 9.
12. Anonymous *Life*, 4:6.
13. W. Brueggemann, *The Bible and Post-modern Imagination* (London: SCM Press, 1993), pp. 24-25.
14. Anonymous *Life*, 2:8.
15. John Killinger, 'Preaching and Silence' in *Lexington Theological Quarterly*, vol. 19, 1984, p. 92.
16. Bede's *Life*, 9.
17. Anonymous *Life*, 3:7 and 4:1.
18. For a fuller treatment of this theme see Alvin C. Rueter, 'Ethics in the Pulpit' in *Word and World*, vol. 8, no. 2, 1988, pp. 173-78.
19. Bede's *Life*, 16.
20. Hans van der Geest, *Presence in the Pulpit* (trans) Douglas W. Stott (Atlanta: John Knox Press, 1981).
21. *Church of England Newspaper*, 24 July 1998.
22. See David Day, 'Preaching the Epistles' in *Anvil*, vol. 14, no. 4, 1997, p. 273 ff.
23. Fred Craddock, *Preaching* (Nashville: Abingdon, 1985), p. 120.
24. Bede's *Life*, 26: 9.

6

RESURRECTING THE SAINTS
HOW CAN THEY INSPIRE US TODAY?

Kate Tristram

The saints we resurrect are the Northern saints of the seventh century: Aidan, Cuthbert, Cedd, Chad, Hild, Ebbe, Wilfrid, Oswald and others. They are sometimes called 'Celtic', though the only one born Celtic was the Irishman Aidan; the others were all 'Anglo-Saxon'. But through Aidan they were all Celtic-trained or Celtic-influenced, and so we can rightly consider the Irish monastic tradition which lay behind their shaping, the tradition that can be seen in the lives of such giants as Columba of Iona. This was carried into much of England by those educated at Lindisfarne and its daughter-houses, and continued to colour English Christianity after the Synod of Whitby had sent the Irish monks back to Iona/Ireland.

We ask: how can they inspire us? We must live in our century, not in theirs, and no one is helped by the sort of historical unrealism that thinks it might be fun to live in a wooden hut on Lindisfarne in the winter! So we avoid romantic nostalgia. Using the sources available we try to see them as they were, and their time as the violent period it was.

Yet they were Christians too, and we can be challenged in our faith and practice as we look at theirs, and in particular at some areas of what is called their 'spirituality', always remembering that they were monks and nuns, the kings excepted, and many of them were first-generation Christians. Naturally their perspectives were different from ours, but their insights and enthusiasms may still find an echo in us. What were these insights?

First, their vivid sense of the reality of God and of his presence. Perhaps this can best be illustrated by what they called 'pilgrimage', which was not quite what we mean by this word. For us a pilgrimage is a planned and often highly organised visit to a place already holy because holy people lived there, or died there, or were seen in visions there; after our visit we go home. For them 'pilgrimage' meant leaving aside all security, taking God's hand and going out: going wherever God led, to do whatever God commanded, never expecting to come home. It was part of their asceticism, their sometimes violent separation from all that hindered their total gift of themselves to God. Such a life was a one-way journey with God who took all the decisions, and so only to be attempted by those who would stake their lives on God's reality. Yet large numbers of monks did so go out – to Iceland, to northern and southern Europe, perhaps to America – to wherever the winds and waves of God took their obedient little boats, there to live and die for their faith.

What about us? Even in our modern world some Christians have so gone out with God. But most of us are in no position to follow literally. Yet we could explore this understanding of pilgrimage as a programme-for-life for all Christians, however fixed their outer environment, if they were prepared to see life as an adventure with God, and in heart and mind to accept all the new challenges and opportunities God puts before each of us.

But how did they know, and what did they know, about this God whom they took so seriously? Here we consider the importance of the Bible. A book culture, reading and writing, came to both Irish and English with Christianity. Before that they had forms of inscriptive writing, ogham and runes, but no books written in their own language. Christian culture was based on Latin, which had to be learned along with reading and writing, and this education could be obtained only in monastic schools. Irish monasteries were passionate about education, and at the heart of Christian education was the Bible.

Of course, very few Christians would ever see a whole Bible, which would be either one huge manuscript or a cupboardful of separate books. Books, handwritten on parchment, were both expensive and heavy. So, in the schools, there was a lot of learning by heart: first the whole of the Book of Psalms, in Latin, which would anchor their prayer-book in the pupils' heads for life; secondly, the Gospels, in Latin, through which Jesus would be both their daily companion and their preaching material; after that sections of the Old Testament; and then the sky was the limit.

The approach was very practical: God gives us his instructions about how we should live. It was also very obedient: there is no arguing with God. Their devotion to the Bible was central to their lives. The contrast with much Christianity nowadays needs pondering.

As they read the Bible they encountered the inescapable human problem: evil. Not only did the Lord suffer opposition and persecution, but he also spoke about Satan and cast out demons. They read of a spiritual warfare, centred in the 'heavenly places', but a war in which we too must fight, though its outcome is not in doubt since Christ has won the decisive battle on the cross. They lived in a warlike society so these ideas would not have been uncongenial, though of course they learnt that spiritual warfare must be fought with the Christian weapons of prayer and fasting, and not with worldly weapons of battle-axe and sword. (Would that all Christians down the ages had learnt this!)

The hermit in particular was called to fight this spiritual battle, relying on God's help alone, and winning spiritual benefits for the whole Church. But all Christians had to resist both the attacks of hostile evil spirits and the moral evil that afflicts humankind. Our saints were realistic and expected their converts to fall many times into the moral mud. So they devised a system whereby, through the help of a spiritual guide, friendly (though often *demanding*) advice could be given. They knew that the way of moral struggle was for many the only way to God, so they taught it, enabled it, and then crowned it with the glory of a special kind of *martyrdom*.

For us too evil is terribly real, though for many Satan and demons are not. Can we approach the problem with the zeal and heroic persistence which they showed?

As they read the Gospels they read also of angels, and thought of them as spiritual beings sent by God to help us on our way to him. Life is a road along which we travel, but there are good companions: angels may take many different forms or be invisible, and some saints, for example St Cuthbert, were more prone to meet them than others, but essentially they aid us on our journey. Other inspiring companions were the earlier saints and martyrs who had gone ahead, but with whom all were united in the Body of Christ. There was also the good company of many 'ordinary' Christians.

What about the non-human creation? They read in Genesis that God had created a harmony before it was disrupted by sin; in Isaiah the visions of the restoration of harmony where the lion can lie down with the lamb; and in the New Testament of the re-creation of all things in Christ when God's Kingdom is revealed and his plan fulfilled. They took the many lovely instances of friendships between saints and wild animals as 'trailers', revealing to us in advance the glory that awaits us in the future, towards which we travel with courage, hope and persistence. In our world, where has this hope gone? Michael Ramsey said 'We do not think enough about heaven', and we need to ask why not.

These four insights are to me among the outstanding characteristics of this version of Christianity. Our saints wrote no books about spirituality, though a few letters and sermons have survived. But others wrote extensively about them, and we have to deduce their thinking, their values, from what they did. Of course many concerns of our society were not theirs. They were not feminists, though in their society as in most others some women had influence. They were not ecologists, though they felt themselves to be part of the whole created world of 'nature' as they met it in the Bible and lived in it in daily life. They sought to spread the faith in an environment very different from ours, but they walked the same tightrope between conforming to 'the world' and confronting it.

If I had to choose one adjective to describe them I would choose 'whole-hearted'. Their commitment to the faith and to the life was impressive indeed, and expressed in generous self-giving and austerity. In case that sounds too grim I borrow a phrase from a scholar, Nora Chadwick, who spent many years studying this material. She asked herself, 'Why do I find them attractive?', and in answer mentioned, among other qualities, their 'spiritual happiness'. That is a further challenge to us, who live alongside so much tense and unhappy religion. Where, for us, shall spiritual happiness be found?

7

GIVING AND RECEIVING SPIRITUAL DIRECTION
WHY SPIRITUAL DIRECTION?

Clare Lockhart

Holman Hunt's famous painting, *The Light of the World*, is perhaps one of the more easily recognised images of Christ in the religious consciousness of recent times. The picture was painted to illustrate one of the most glorious gifts of the Christian life, the promise of the Risen Christ in the third chapter of the Book of Revelation.

> Here I am! I stand at the door and knock. If anyone hears my voice and opens the door, I will come in and eat with him and he with me.[1]

Every Christian is given the possibility of a direct and intimate relationship with the holy and immortal God. The promise made by Christ is of a warm and homely presence at the heart of our life, a place of shelter and peace, a joyful communion, as between father, mother and child, between brother and sister or lover and beloved. The progress of our lives through time and space in the world is mirrored by a journey within, where the door to the world of eternity and grace is always open, and where nothing can mar or hinder the sweetness and cordiality of our friendship with God.

What then is the theological basis for a doctrine of spiritual direction, of human intervention in this most profound and sacred union? Can we not rely solely on the Holy Spirit to be our guide? If, however, we look again at Holman Hunt's painting, we may see a paradox. The door, at which Christ knocks, is fast shut, surrounded by thorns and brambles. Christ himself stands in a landscape of autumnal gloom and dispirited neglect. Which then is the outer, and which the inner world? Is he somewhere 'outside' in the world knocking at the door of the spirit for the first time, the one within beguiled by the glamour of the world, deaf, with the heedlessness of youth, to the call of the stranger outside?

Or is the orchard itself, with its storm-bowed trees and fallen apples, symbolic of the inner reaches of the human heart, perhaps the heart of one long weary of the Christian journey, whose spiritual state is echoed in the words of Shakespeare:

> That time of year thou may'st in me behold
> When yellow leaves or none or few do hang
> Against those boughs that shake against the cold
> Bare ruin'd choirs, where late the sweet birds sang.[2]

Dante, in the opening lines of the 'Inferno', describes the predicament of midlife crisis:

> In the middle of the journey of our life
> I found myself in a dark wood
> Having lost the straight path.

These lines are echoed in T. S. Eliot's description of middle age in 'East Coker':

> In the middle, not only in the middle of the way
> But all the way, in a dark wood, in a bramble,
> On the edge of a grimpen, where there is no secure foothold,
> And menaced by monsters, fancy lights,
> Risking enchantment.

Christ knocks, but the house of the spirit is perhaps untenanted, the soul gone in search of evasion or distraction from the demands of the spiritual life.

Nevertheless, middle age, often the time when we experience that boredom and lack of enthusiasm for the things of God which the medieval writers called *accidie*, can be a time of a second 'conversion', of finding oneself, even if it is only to find that one is lost.

In Russell Hoban's novel about the post-nuclear world, Ridley Walker, the eponymous hero, finds the wreckage of mysterious buildings. It is a moment of illumination as he realises that he and his fellows are the descendants of those who designed and built those amazing constructions that are no more. 'Oh what we come to and what we been,' he weeps.

As we look into the face of Christ and meditate on his life, we too weep as we realise how far from the image of God we have come. Like the Prodigal Son, we come to ourselves. This realisation is itself the work of the Holy Spirit deep within us. However, we need to be brought to the point where we can see ourselves more clearly in the light of Christ.

Receiving Spiritual Direction

Any Christian who begins to 'find himself' and desires seriously to respond to the inner call of Christ, will probably soon be in need of advice or guidance in the spiritual life. Most of us need help as we adjust the eyes of the spirit to the new landscape in which we find ourselves. As for any journey, we need a map of the terrain, from those who have themselves undertaken the journey home with all its challenges and pitfalls. But before we begin the journey ourselves, we need to make an honest appraisal of our life so far, reflecting in a prayerful way upon who we are and where we have come from.

Exercise: Knowing Myself

This is a simple exercise, which can help to give us an historical overview of our spiritual life.

On a blank sheet of paper you can make a graphic map of your life so far.

- First, mark off the decades on the vertical axis and the years of the decades on the horizontal axis.

- Now highlight, in colour, either in writing or in some personal code, the experiences or relationships which you think have had a significant influence upon your life in an enhancing or affirming way.
- Using a different colour, put in the darker experiences or relationships, those which perhaps have scarred you or left you vulnerable.
- Mark in the times of spiritual quickening, when you felt a sense of God's hand in your life or a quickening of your faith.
- Turn the paper over.
- Write down the things about yourself or your past life that you are sorry for, or that you wish were different.
- Write down your aspirations, both the person you would like to be, and the person you think God would like you to be. Identify any conflict there may be there.
- Make a list of the things that you feel are hindering your spiritual progress.

Baron Von Hugel, an eminent Roman Catholic writer of the nineteenth century, used the phrase 'spiritual attrait' to describe the way in which Christians are drawn to different spiritual paths. This perhaps is only another way of saying that each of us has a different charism or gift from the Holy Spirit.

Some Christians have a passion for social justice as their primary spiritual attrait; others see contemplative prayer or preaching and teaching as the most important activity in their life.

- In the final part of this exercise write down which area of Christian life and witness you see as your primary spiritual attrait and the corresponding gifts which God has given you.

Why We Need Spiritual Direction

This exercise of reflecting on our life map and spiritual history can help us focus more clearly on our journey ahead as we recognise and acknowledge both our strength and our vulnerability. The exercise may have been painful. Perhaps we are left with a nagging sense of insecurity about ourselves. The memory of past failures or hurts may have disturbed us. We may be conscious of a lack of fulfilment in our lives, a sense of regret at opportunities missed or uneasiness about the direction that our life has taken. We may find that we are uncertain of our future direction or fearful of treading the wrong path. If this is so, and if, after prayerful reflection, we find the way ahead is still clouded by the shadows of the past, we may need the kindly perspective of a spiritual friend to help us perceive, to make a discerning judgement about where we are and how we stand in the sight of God. Perhaps the time has come for us to look beyond our own resources and seek direction.

Non-judgmental listening and the process of reflecting back have become the most desirable qualities in contemporary forms of pastoral care. But the role of the spiritual director goes beyond simple listening. One of the greatest hindrances to progress in the spiritual life is unreality, and underlying this may be a reluctance to be honest with ourselves. The fruits of the spirit grow in the rich soil of penitence washed by the tears of the sinner. It may be possible to foster a kind of spirituality which is not rooted in that sorrow for sin which is the ground of all spiritual endeavour, but the end of such is like the rootless tumbleweeds in the Nevada desert travelling aimlessly in all directions and bearing no fruit.

The most helpful quality in a spiritual director then at the beginning of our journey home is a compassionate discernment, which can make a judgement about the state of our life from the perspective, not of a disinterested observer, but of someone whose concern is for our spiritual progress, whose loving interference can perhaps enable us to come to ourselves more truthfully. In the next section we will consider the various ways in which this has been found in the past.

Some Important Strands In The History Of Spiritual Direction

Within the Christian tradition people have sought spiritual

guidance from many different sources, reflecting the variety of traditions within the Church. At the heart of this search is a sense of the spiritual life as an apprenticeship, of knowledge passed on from one experienced in the ways and means of the life of prayer and growth in holiness. So the Desert Fathers in their solitude were visited by students of the ascetic life, drawn in their thousands by the lives of those for whom contemplative prayer was an end in itself, who saw there the purity and simplicity of a life lived solely for God and stayed to share the vision. This life of contemplative prayer and penance re-emerged in the lives of the monks and nuns of the Celtic Church who set up their beehive cells in the wildest and most remote corners of Ireland, Wales and the Western Isles. The link between the Fathers of the desert and the early Celtic monastic tradition is attested by the various representations of St Anthony and St Paul the hermit in Pictish art.

At St Vigean's in Dundee a seventh-century Pictish stone depicts the first meeting of the two hermits as recounted in *The Life of St Paul the Hermit* by St Jerome. When they sat to break bread, such was their humility and respect one for the other that neither would say grace and be the first to break the bread. They then agreed to place the bread in the centre of the table and pull it at the same time, and it is this moment that is captured on the stone, illustrating for us the poise and balance of the 'soul friend'.

Similarly, the great monastic foundations of the Western Church were centres of spiritual formation for generations of medieval Christians. Their descending hierarchies of membership within the household – choir monks and nuns, lay brothers and sisters, tertiaries and child oblates – all bore the hallmark of their spiritual founder. In particular, the central motif of monastic spirituality, the Opus Dei, the Divine Office, was echoed by the laity with their Primers and Books of Hours, was noted even by the peasants in the fields as they heard the bells mark out the cyclic chronology of liturgical time. This motif passed into the religious consciousness of the generations so that even after the Reformation when the Mass itself was displaced from the heart of the new religion, the tradition of Common Prayer still persisted in the lives of the laity, finding its locus in the parish church.

In the Catholic tradition of the Church, spiritual direction in the lives of the laity came to be associated with the sacrament of confession and therefore was seen primarily as a priestly ministry. The Counter-Reformation saw a renaissance of spiritual direction formed and guided by parish clergy. For example, in seventeenth-century France, Vincent de Paul and Louise de Marillac were pioneers in encouraging new forms of women's ministry in the Church and in framing alternative, non-monastic models of the Christian life for clergy and laity. The Congregation of the Mission was a band of secular clergy who shared a rule of life adapted to their role as pastors in the city. Later their ministry extended to the neglected peasant classes in the rural parishes. In founding the Daughters of Charity, Vincent and Louise broke new ground in enabling simple country girls to minister to people of their own class, unfettered by the customary enclosure of the religious of the time. They made annual promises of renewal rather than simple or solemn vows and the tenor of their life was expressed most eloquently in the words of the Rule, which declared that the Daughter of Charity was to have:

> For convent the house of suffering, for cell some poor lodging, for chapel the parish church; for cloister the streets of the city or the wards of the hospital, for enclosure obedience; for bolts and bars the fear of God; and for veil, holy modesty.[4]

The spiritual formation of the community was effected primarily by the monthly Conferences upon the Rule convened by Vincent and Louise. Vincent would raise a question of faith or practice from the Rule and each sister was encouraged to share her thoughts on the subject under discussion. The Conferences are marked by a deeply practical spirituality inspired by the community life of the young Church in Acts. The emphasis on the primacy of charity over religious exercises is reflected in the direction in the Rule:

> In urgent need, put the service of the poor in the first place even before your religious exercises, for in so doing you only leave God to find God.[5]

This is in deep contrast to the Rule of St Benedict, 'Let nothing be preferred to the Work of God'. It marks a paradigm shift in the understanding of spirituality from a milieu in which the normative ideal is monastic, contemplative and celibate, to an ideal exemplified by communities inspired by the evangelical counsels, both Catholic and Protestant; from the various orders of Friars to the Bruderhof communities and Beguinages of the Low Countries. By the seventeenth century, significantly perhaps, it was within the Christian family that the primary locus of spirituality began to be seen, the idea that growth in holiness was possible in the everyday fulfilment of the duties of one's state of life. The ideal of the penitential self-denial of the ascetic began to be replaced by a kinder theology of domestic grace, epitomised in the words of George Herbert, the Anglican poet and Rector of Bemerton near Salisbury:

> Teach me my God and king
> In all things Thee to see
> And what I do in anything
> To do it as for Thee.

> The servant with this clause
> Makes drudgery divine
> Who sweeps a room as for thy sake
> Makes that and the action fine.[6]

The authenticity of a genuinely lay spirituality which could find 'heaven in the ordinary' was complemented by the way in which Anglican and Puritan divines increasingly saw their pastoral duty as including spiritual direction. The writings of men like Samuel Rutherford and John Owen as well as William Laud and Jeremy Taylor provide us with evidence that at least in the ideal, the parish priest or pastor was the main source of spiritual guidance for the laity in the Anglican and Puritan traditions.

Two hundred years later, F. P. Harton, sometime chaplain to the Anglican Community of Sisters of Charity at Knowle in Bristol and later Dean of Wells, was to write on this topic in his classic work *The Elements of The Spiritual Life:*

> Spiritual Direction is not the close preserve of a few experts, but an essential part of the responsibility of every priest with the cure of souls.... . The priest's whole ability to guide souls depends on his being a man of God. Spiritual guidance can only be undertaken by one who is himself humbly seeking to live with and for God: A worldly priest though he may be popular is incapable for this work; nor is it sufficient merely to have a good knowledge of human nature, nor to be well up in the latest theories of psychology. The direction of souls is the work of the Holy Spirit, and the priest is simply the human medium through whom the spirit works. The priest treats souls on the spiritual level and what is important for him is an adequate knowledge of the four closely related branches of theology – dogmatic, moral, ascetical and mystical. Of these we would stress the third, which should be studied not in little books, but in the works of the proven masters.[7]

Sixty years later we shall probably give more credence than did Harton to the latest theories of psychology. The study of all the social sciences, the work of Frank Lake in the Clinical Theology movement and the theories of counselling in our own time have provided in their several ways a creative and fruitful catalyst to theological exploration. Most courses offered on spiritual direction or the spiritual life contain some elements of psychology or counselling theory. But the burden of his song in relation to the need for the director to be primarily a man (or woman) of God is echoed as a spiritual health warning by Kenneth Leech in an article in *The Tablet* in May 1993 where he questions the trend towards marketing and popularising the role of the spiritual director:

> Directors play quite a lowly and limited function within the wider context of pastoral care and theological formation. Spiritual Direction is not essentially a ministry for specialists and professionals but part of the ordinary pastoral ministry of every parish and every Christian.... The role of training is extremely limited and this ministry is essentially a by-product of a life of prayer and growth in holiness.[8]

In spite of Leech's warning, in contemporary Church life the art of spiritual direction is very much an issue for anyone involved in ministry, as its inclusion in a book of this kind might indicate.

Finding Spiritual Guidance

The varying models of spiritual guidance described in the review above are all available to us today. The exercise in this chapter was designed to focus on yourself and your spiritual needs. As we moved through that swift review of the main pathways of spiritual direction, you may have been attracted by the description of a particular group, depending on your own spiritual 'attrait' and what you feel you are needing to address in your spiritual life.

Perhaps in the frenetic round of your daily commitments you long for some experience of the eternal peace. Benedictine life has continued in an unbroken and often unmodified tradition for fifteen hundred years to witness to the original vision of its founder:

the tranquillity of order, the primacy of common prayer in the formation of the monastic character and the values of learning and hospitality. The abbeys and priories usually have guest houses where it is possible to stay and share for a time in the life of the Order, going to the Divine Office, helping with the work of the house or speaking to one of the monks or nuns about the life of the spirit.

Maybe your particular passion is for the environment, and you are attracted by the Celtic vision of the green martyrdom. The Celtic vision is of a land-based spirituality which celebrates the interlinking of all creation in a warm familiarity of kinship, and the hallowing of the very least of all activities by prayer. In the communities of Iona and Fetlar we find lived out in contemporary style the old ideal of the *chaim*, the circle of friends bound to each other, some remaining in the place of prayer, others moving to a life of journeying and pilgrimage. And if we are true to the Celtic vision, we shall not forget the place of penitence in the life of the Celtic monks, the nights spent weeping for their sins, the long fasts and times of discipline.

Wherever it is that we find our spiritual home, whether it be Taizé or Bec or Iona, or a Franciscan friary, a cell group in the city or a barn in the Western Isles, there we will find companions on the way, a loving community of countless pilgrims with faces turned homeward to the heavenly city. Somewhere in that great company we may find a soul friend to break the bread of tears of penitence, to share the wine of spiritual joy. But at the very heart of our life there will always be the secret reality of Christ's promise in John:

> If anyone loves me he will obey my teaching. My Father will love him, and we will come to him, and make our home with him.[9]

NOTES

1. Revelation 3:20.
2. William Shakespeare, Sonnet 73, *Collected Works*.

3. Quoted in T. S. Eliot, *Four Quartets*, Bernard Bergonzi (ed.), p. 45.
4. Quoted in *The Rule of the Sisters of Charity*, Private Imprint, p. 29.
5. Ibid., p. 40.
6. *Hymns Ancient and Modern*, no. 337.
7. Quoted in Peter Ball, *Journey into Truth: Spiritual Direction in the Anglican Tradition* (London: Mowbray, 1996).
8. Ibid., 'Is spiritual direction losing its bearings?' in *The Tablet*, 22 May 1993, p. 95.
9. John 14:23.

APPENDIX: GIVING AND RECEIVING SPIRITUAL GUIDANCE

You may find the following exercises useful:

Exercise 1
The list below contains some of the elements and qualities that have characterised the tradition of spiritual guidance within the Christian tradition. Assign to each element a number, according to its importance to you in your own spiritual life:

- sacramental confession
- counselling qualification
- non-judgemental listening
- experienced in contemplative prayer and meditation
- ability to discern and understand
- personal friendship
- ability to confront and challenge
- theological qualification

Exercise 2
On our spiritual journey the Holy Spirit guides us in many ways. Some of these sources are listed here. Make a 'pie chart'. Divide the pie into slices to show the proportional significance in your life of:

- Spiritual reading
- Prayer groups
- Personal prayer
- Holy Scripture
- Advice from friends and family
- Parish priest
- Designated spiritual director

Exercise 3

Why would anyone need a spiritual director? Rate the following in order of attractiveness:

- A spiritual director personally guides me in my prayer life, recommends spiritual reading and is there for me as a mentor in life crises, or when I need advice about major decisions.
- A soul friend shares my spiritual journey. We are mutually affirming and encouraging. We are honest with each other about our failings and we share spiritual insights.
- I make a sacramental confession four times a year and have a chat with the priest about prayer and my daily life. I have always been attracted to contemplative spirituality and sometimes visit a monastery/convent where I can talk to one of the monks/nuns about prayer.
- I belong to a prayer group in the parish. We have Bible studies and quiet evenings and often share our experiences. If I had a problem I would tell the group. We support each other by prayer.

SING FOR GOD'S GLORY

Sing for God's glory
that colours the dawn of creation
racing across the sky,
trailing bright clouds of elation;
sun of delight succeeds the velvet of night,
warming the earth's exultation.

Sing for God's power
that shatters the chains that would bind us,
searing the darkness of fear
and despair that could blind us,
touching our shame with love that will not lay blame,
reaching out gently to find us.

Sing for God's justice
disturbing each easy illusion,
tearing down tyrants
and putting our pride to confusion;
lifeblood of right, resisting evil and slight,
offering freedom's transfusion.

Sing for God's saints who have
travelled faith's journey before us,
who in our weariness
give us their hope to restore us;
in them we see the new creation to be,
spirit of love made flesh for us.

Words: Kathy Galloway
Music: Lobe den Herren, arranged Panel on Worship,
Wild Goose Publications

A COLLECT FOR SAINT CUTHBERT'S DAY
(20 MARCH)

Almighty God,
who didst call thy servant Cuthbert from keeping sheep
to follow thy Son and to be a shepherd of thy people,
mercifully grant that we,
following his example and caring for those who are lost,
may bring them home to thy fold,
through thy Son Jesus Christ our Lord.
Amen.

PART FOUR
LAY MISSIONARY LEADERSHIP FOR A NEW MILLENNIUM

8

READERS AND MISSIONARY LEADERSHIP FOR A NEW MILLENNIUM

The text of a sermon preached by the Right Reverend Christopher Mayfield at the Central Readers' Council National Conference Eucharist, in the Chapel of the College of St Hild and St Bede, Durham University

Text: Luke 14:25-34

> For which of you, intending to build a tower, does not first sit down and estimate the cost to see whether you have enough to complete it?... In the same way, none of you can become my disciple if you do not give up all your possessions.

The Gospel reading captures something of the tension between Benedictine Rule and Celtic spirituality; the discipline of counting the cost alongside the seeming foolishness of giving all.

As with many of Jesus' sayings and teachings, both need to be heard; they need to be held together. Both, 'the counting of the cost' and 'the giving of all', are true.

Wallace and Grommit might be thought of as one example of Celtic spirituality meeting Benedictine Rule. Those northern, Oscar-winning, animated characters, created by Nick Park from Preston in Lancashire, typify one result of combining the contrasting characteristics of the regulated and balanced life of Benedictine communities, with their emphasis on prayer, work and learning, and the freer, more fluid expression of spirituality, which often went to extremes in Celtic communities.

In Wallace we see a gentle man who drifts through life. He bumbles along without much idea of where he is going, but has inventions to order and regulate every aspect of his life.

Unfortunately his 'Heath Robinson' type contraptions often go disastrously wrong with hilarious results. It is a life of extreme regulation, achieving very little. It is also a life of disorder, without direction. His dog, Grommit, fortunately has more common sense, and always manages to save the day.

Today there is a deep interest in all things Celtic. This is a time of great spiritual searching. Our role as members of Christ's Church is to get alongside those outside the Church, to offer, in Christ, a way that allows for the joy and spontaneity of an individual's spiritual awakening, yet provides a framework within which that awakening can be nurtured in purity, love and truth (Poverty, Chastity and Obedience). This way of approaching the meeting of Celtic spirituality and Benedictine Rule should prove more effective than that of Wallace and Grommit.

In the Church of England, licensed Readers have a key role to play in providing leadership in such missionary activity which is part of the ministry of the whole body of the Church. Let me suggest three areas in which they could make a great difference: in Creating Community; Thinking Theology; and Moving Mission.

1. Creating Community

One of the lessons that today's Church is learning from both Celtic and Benedictine forms of monasticism is the importance of life as community. Less emphasis on the individual, more on the communal and mutual dimension of ministry.

Monasticism in the Western Church, in both its Celtic and Benedictine expressions, had its origins in the so-called Egyptian Desert Fathers. They were people who felt so strongly the need to live a life of holiness, that they left 'the world' behind in order to pursue a life of prayer, holiness and deepening spiritual understanding. I say so-called Desert 'Fathers' because, in fact, many of these monks were lay people; and, indeed, some were women!

Martin of Tours, a Roman soldier converted to Christianity,

brought the monastic way of life to Gaul. From Gaul, the monastic tradition travelled west to Britain and then to Ireland with the influence of Ninian and Illtyd. Here it flourished. On mainland Europe the monastic ideal was to flounder in the midst of political, religious and social upheaval. Christianity became increasingly materialistic and decadent. It took on the structures of the empire it served.

On the Continent, it was to be more than a century before Benedict was to establish a successful monastic system at Monte Cassino. The Benedictine community life brought a fresh missionary zeal to the Roman Church. At the same time Columbanus was bringing the Irish monastic system back to France.

Ireland, unlike continental Europe and Britain, had never come under Roman Imperial rule. It remained a rural rather than an urban economy. This was well suited to those seeking a way of life separate from 'the world'. In the Celtic expression of Christianity the concept of 'community' was so strong that even those monks who lived as hermits, away from all other human contact, found themselves building community with the wild creatures of forest, rivers and sea. Saint Colman had three such companions – a cockerel, a mouse and a fly. The cock would crow to wake Colman for the first Office of the early hours; the mouse would gnaw at his feet to wake him later in the morning; and the fly would crawl across his Bible, marking the correct place for his reading of scripture.

And stories abound, of otters or seals warming the feet and body of St Cuthbert after a night up to his neck in the river or sea in prayer. His mortal remains are buried in Durham Cathedral. It is not surprising that the groups which have had the biggest influence on Church life in recent years have been community-based. Taizé, Iona, the House Church movement have each, in their own way, had an impact on the way in which many Church of England congregations live and work. Courses such as Alpha, Emmaus and Credo have been successful, largely because of their emphasis on the building of community among their members. It is good that in many parishes, Readers have had an active part in the leadership of these courses.

There is a growing interest in the Cell Church Movement. This has its origins in the Latin American experience of basic Christian communities, and has been adapted to many cultures around the world from Mongolia to Manchester!

In a Home Cell Group, through positive relationships with other Christians, a caring and encouraging environment can be experienced. There is mutual pastoral ministry. From these things, a natural outreach to the circle of friends, family, neighbours and workmates of members flows.

The mission statement of one of the parish churches in Manchester Diocese which is introducing Cell groups is, '*To be disciples of Jesus in order to make disciples for Jesus*'. Their vicar writes:

> Groups of no more than twelve to fifteen committed members meet weekly, not just for Bible study and prayer, but to share in the spiritual and pastoral care of one another. A cell group is the church living in community. It is a basic Christian community of God's people, spanning ages and interests, brought together by Christ because they belong to his Church, in order to live out their Christian lives in practical ways under the leadership of the Holy Spirit. Being Church in a different way to that which is experienced by most on Sunday mornings.[1]

In many of the parishes where Cell churches are being established, it is Readers who lead and resource them.

Creating community is an essential part of the missionary task today. A rediscovery of what it means to live in community, helping those who often feel excluded to be included within the Church of Christ, could have the same impact today as it had fifteen hundred years ago. Just as the Celtic saints brought light back into the lives of those living in the dark ages of our history, we can bring that same light of Christ into dark places of our society today.

2. Thinking Theology

In addition to creating community I believe that Readers are called to think theologically and to do so as lay ministers.

We meet at a time when the Church is desperately calling for more priests. To meet the need for priestly ministry there has been a rapid rise in the growth of both non-stipendiary ministry, accredited both nationally and locally, through various schemes for ordained local ministry.

Many Readers express feelings of concern regarding the future of Reader ministry. There have been calls to ordain Readers, or to use Readers as lay presidents at the Eucharist. With confidence in the ministry of lay people, we need to resist these pressures. Baptism, not ordination, is the initiation into discipleship and ministry. All are called to proclaim the Good News of the Kingdom; to encourage new believers; to respond to human need by loving service; to work for justice in society; to strive to safeguard the integrity of creation; and to sustain and renew the earth. Readers can and should be those who lead the way in opportunities for active and informed lay ministry in today's Church, just as in past generations the ministry and mission of Church was largely lay-led in both Celtic and Benedictine communities.

Lay leadership was crucial to both Celtic and Benedictine communities. Both alike were governed by an abbot or abbess who was often not ordained. The Rule of St Benedict Chapter LXII gives instructions for the exercise of priesthood: 'If an Abbot wishes to have a priest or deacon ordained for his service, he should choose from his monks one who is fit to exercise the priesthood. He who is ordained, however, must beware of elation or pride and he should not take upon himself any work that has not been committed to him by the Abbot.'[2]

The Celtic system, in particular, was not based around the

authority of a bishop in his city (or the priest in his parish) but around the authority of abbot or abbess and the 'mission field' of the community.

Thinking theology is not the preserve of the ordained. Licensed Readers have a unique place in the Church as it exists Monday to Saturday dispersed in the wider community of our society: in places of work; schools; offices; the factory floor. Lay people, yet with training in biblical studies and pastoral care, have the privilege to be able to 'think theology' in places where people are, where the pulse of the nation can be felt, day by day, week in and week out.

Rhoda Hiscox, in her book, *Celebrating Reader Ministry*, published to celebrate the 125th anniversary of Reader ministry in 1991, spoke of her dream:

> I dream of Readers taking initiatives with other Christians and with those outside the Church, exploring topics in, for example, the fields of medical, legal or business ethics, or engaging in radical thinking and political action in relation to issues of peace and justice and other areas of life where Christian values are threatened. I dream of Readers sufficiently competent and confident in their faith, theology and skills of communication, to work outside the institutional Church in lives of risk-taking and vulnerability. Just before waking I dream that some Readers are being welcomed as trainers of clergy in theological colleges and courses, in continuing ministerial education and in training courses for archdeacons and bishops.[3]

Bishop Alec Graham, the former Bishop of Newcastle, had a dream of licensed Readers as the lay theologians of the Church, men and women who could relate theology to their daily life and tasks, breaking down the false barrier that seems to have been created between the so-called sacred and secular aspects of our life.

The Celtic Christians were renowned for their understanding of the human place in creation. Not above it, as Lords, nor even as stewards, but at one with it. They recognised that the human vocation was to both share in God's delight in the created order, and to articulate the creation's praise of God by its order, beauty and sheer exuberance. So a poem of praise to God, recorded in the Black Book of Carmarthen, reads thus:

> I am the wind that breathes upon the sea,
> I am the wave on the ocean,
> I am the murmur of the leaves rustling,
> I am the rays of the sun,
> I am the beam of the moon and the stars,
> I am the power of trees growing,
> I am the bud breaking into blossom,
> I am the movement of the salmon swimming,
> I am the courage of the wild boar fighting,
> I am the speed of the stag running,
> I am the strength of the ox pulling the plough,
> I am the size of the mighty oak tree,
> And I am the thoughts of all people
> Who praise my beauty and grace.[4]

They saw no distinction between sacred and secular. Prayers for lighting the fire, milking the cow and weaving cloth show something of the way in which they thought theologically about their daily existence and every aspect of life.

The Rule of St Benedict emphasised the importance of an integrated life, one in which the 'Work of God' (prayer), 'The work of the hands' (our daily occupation), and 'spiritual reading' (study) each complemented the other.

We can do the same today. Readers, in particular, with their training in theological reflection, should be making the connections between what they know and are learning from theological training and their daily experiences; thinking theology and bridging the huge gap between the culture of Church and the cultures that make up our society.

3. Moving Mission

In helping to 'create community' and to 'think theology' Readers have an opportunity to 'move the mission' of the Church.

The Benedictine system of a stable monastic life, under the authority of a bishop based at his city *cathedra,* suited the more settled 'Christian' situation of Southern Italy. The settled diocesan and parochial system of the Church of England grew out of that system. The advantages are great. Every inch of England is in one of our 12,000 or so parishes. Every person in England lives in an area in which pastoral care is, at least in theory, provided for all.

The Church of England has been very good at a ministry of maintenance within such a settled Christian society. For many centuries it has been good at *maintaining* pastoral contact with the community. Even now, people turn to the Church of England for baptisms, weddings and funerals. But for many years there has been a growing gap in the understanding of these occasional offices between members of the committed Christian community and others in our society. Now we see that gap of understanding resulting in decreasing demand for these pastoral offices. Fewer babies are now brought for baptism, fewer weddings take place at all, let alone in church. Now people are looking at alternative funeral arrangements. So called 'green' burials and secular ceremonies, focused entirely on the deceased and the bereaved, without reference to God and the Christian hope of resurrection, are increasingly sought after. Despite all our efforts at maintenance, if we look at the statistics we see that the structure is beginning to break down. The settled Christian society which the Church has served is becoming a thing of the past.

The Celtic way suited the more missionary situation of pagan Britain. Christianity spread very rapidly in Britain through the development of monastic communities of the Celtic tradition. A

Celtic monastery under the authority of an abbot seemed to have operated along similar sociological lines to that of the Celtic tribal system. The chief or king had the responsibility for all his family, members of the group or clan; they in turn had duties and functions, at his disposal, used for the mutual benefit of the group.

As a monastery grew, the Abbot would often appoint leaders of bands of wanderers and send out members to found new communities elsewhere. These *peregrinati* were at the cutting edge of mission and ministry. They were frowned upon by Benedictines, who valued the importance of stability. The Rule of St Benedict is scathing:

> They are never stable throughout their whole lives but wanderers through diverse regions, receiving hospitality in the monastic cells of others for three or four days at a time. Always roving and never settling, they follow their own wills, enslaved by the attractions of gluttony… it is better to pass over in silence than to speak of the unhappy way of life of all these people (chapter 1).[5]

But the *peregrinati* were crucial to the rapid spread of Christianity in the Celtic Mission. Benedict never travelled further than the sixty miles from his hermitage in Nursia to Monte Cassino, where he established the monastery that was to have such an influence on the development of community life. But Celtic leaders like Brendan, Columba and Columbanus thought nothing of crossing seas, mountains and forests, to take the Christian message to the furthest bounds of the known world.

Perhaps the reason for the failure of Paulinus' Roman Mission to Northumbria was his reluctance to leave the royal household. St Aidan, on his arrival from Iona, settled not in the royal palace at Bamburgh, but on the Island of Lindisfarne, better known by the people of Northumbria still as Holy Island. From there the gospel was brought to the ordinary people of the outlying rural communities of the kingdom. We need to move from maintenance mode to missionary mode; to look outward to the communities we serve, and discover fresh ways of offering compassionate love.

I have had the privilege of visiting a variety of Church Urban Fund projects in Manchester Diocese. Each, in its own way, manages to combine both a response to human need by loving service and a proclamation of the Good News of the Kingdom of God. One of the great achievements of many CUF projects has been the building of a real sense of community in places where community is all but lost. The loss of a sense of community is true in both urban and rural settings. In many cities and in isolated rural areas there is an increasing sense of alienation from the consumer world of today. Unemployment levels may be falling, but for those who are now the third or fourth generation out-of-work, personally it is, still, one hundred per cent. Grinding poverty has resulted in a dependency culture for many and a crime culture for others.

In many rural areas, dormitorisation of villages has broken down the old sense of community with a new breed of resident: commuters, holiday-makers and weekend residents, and the relatively new phenomenon of the electronic commuter – those working in the 'high-tech' or financial industries, from even the most remote parts of our land, from their home computer, using the electronic super-highway of the worldwide web. The rural idyll of real community life is no longer, if it ever really existed at all.

Rebuilding a sense of community is surely one of the most important ways in which we can respond, both to the human need of those who live in our parishes and to the challenge of the individualistic structures of modern society.

In such a situation, a synthesis of both the Celtic and Benedictine strands can be called upon to our advantage. The medieval minster was something of such a synthesis, a half-way house, as Bishop John Finney describes them, between the Celtic community set in a pagan kingdom and the Roman ideal of a parish priest in every place.

These minsters were semi-monastic mother churches with a strong evangelistic emphasis on planting churches and Christian communities in the surrounding area. Usually the bishop, rather than an abbot, was in charge, and from a minster, a wide area could be ministered to by his clergy and lay team, evangelising the places that were still pagan, and caring for those areas which had become Christian.[6]

The mission of the Church proved very successful with a minster model of ministry. A new minster has recently been established in nearby Sunderland, perhaps the first new minster to be created for centuries. We can hope and pray that it too will bring a fresh sense of mission and ministry in the communities it serves. There is much to commend of the minster model, but we need to take care to avoid slavishly sticking to it. We should still allow for a little Celtic openness and fluidity.

As the local Church today accepts responsibility to minister the gospel in its own area, there are implications for the partnership between stipendiary clergy and other members of the local expression of the Body of Christ. There will need to be real collaboration in ministry; clergy and lay people; and clergy and other clergy really working together for the good of all they serve.

It is over twenty years since Canon John Tiller proposed that the ministers, lay and ordained, of a Deanery should be seen to work as a ministry team, the area/rural dean having oversight of a team of other clergy and of lay ministers, including licensed Readers. This is a 'modified minster' model. The stress is not on the building from which the mission and ministry is directed, nor on the 'status' of the ministers concerned within the Ministry Team, but on the community which is being served.

For the local Church is not the building in which it meets, but a Christian community, a household of faith. New households can be built, in new contexts which transcend our existing parish boundaries, for example the development of services aimed at young people, the growth of Christian cell groups and the gathering of those engaged in particular tasks of service. Building community, thinking through theology and making connections with daily life becomes so attractive that others are drawn in to discover, sometimes refresh, sometimes for the first time, what God's loving purposes can mean for them. The Church moves from a preoccupation with maintenance and becomes focused on its mission.

In this task, Readers are our new *peregrinati*. Their role will often be misunderstood, even despised. Lay ministers are on the edges of Christian ministry. Their role as lay leaders is not only in the gathered Church community, but in their accessibility to a wider fringe, with a particular task to fulfil in places of work, leisure, and community involvement. Readers are creating community, thinking theology and moving mission, despite the structures and strictures of the institutional Church.

As St Paul says to Philemon, 'I pray that you may be active in sharing your faith, so that you will have a full understanding of every good thing that we have in Christ.'

One of the adventures in which Wallace and Grommit feature, is the incident of the 'Wrong Trousers'. Wallace inadvertently puts on a pair of mechanical trousers which will not respond to his control. They run amok, causing chaos. We need to make sure that the Church is wearing the right trousers; trousers that fit the missionary task in hand today. I see a Church emerging that values the ministry of everyone, ordained and lay, less dependent on the availability of a large number of stipendiary clergy, depending instead on the willingness of lay people to wake up to their calling, their ministry, their mission. In this, the training and ministry of licensed Readers will play a central part. I see a Church in which Celtic spirituality and Benedictine Rule have met and embraced each other with overflowing joy and with sincerity of heart. A Church with enough fluidity to respond to the rapidly changing circumstances of our world today, yet with enough order and stability to keep us together as we travel the pilgrim way.

For however strong our Benedictine tendency to remain with the familiar and to long for stability, there is no doubt in my mind that as Christians we are called, like the Celtic saints of old, to move ever onward on a wonderful discovery of God in the things that are new and fresh. Bringing from the treasure store, as Jesus said, things that are both old and new (Matthew 13:52).

NOTES

1. Peter Leakey, *An Introduction to Cell Church* (PCC discussion paper).
2. David Parry, *The Rule of St Benedict* (DLT, 1984), p. 98.
3. Rhoda Hiscox, *Celebrating Reader Ministry* (Mowbray, 1991), p. 481.
4. Robert Van de Weyer, *Celtic Fire* (DLT, 1990), p. 92.
5. Op.cit., p. 7.
6. John Finney, *Recovering the Past* (DLT, 1996) p. 113-41.

A REFLECTION ON MISSION

Alison White

Mission is characterised by Five Marks:

To proclaim the Good News of the Kingdom.
To teach, baptise and nurture new believers.
To respond to human need by loving service.
To seek to transform unjust structures of society.
To strive to safeguard the integrity of creation and sustain and renew the earth.

(The Anglican Consultative Council)

Mission?

It is a word with baggage
Which is often heavy, loaded, encumbering.
We carry guilt
and a sense of 'ought to'.

Yet
Mission is not about new tasks,
Mission is in the nature of God.
We cannot opt in or out of it.

Therefore
It is about both knowing God – and making Him known.
It is both response and responsibility.
It is about the whole of us
corporately and individually
in who we are
what we do
and what we say.

Mission is Local

'Local' is different for each of us.
It is the place where we are now.
It is the object of God's love.
It is the arena of His activity.

Therefore
Incarnation is central to our understanding of engagement.
By Incarnation God engages directly with us
through the body, mind and soul of Jesus.
Through his Spirit we engage
in his name
locally!

If there is such a thing as a sacred place,
where we may hope to encounter God;
then we must search locally
and expect to find the 'Holy'
close at hand.

Lay Ministry is Local Mission

The Lay Minister (often the Reader in the Church of England) becomes eyes, ears and mouth, observing, contemplating, reflecting on life in the community, at work, in Church, in God.

For those who preach, or contribute to discussion groups, or are called to speak in any way, there is the necessity to speak about what they have discovered or observed. But, reader (Reader) note well:

All must be kept in fitting proportion,
two eyes, two ears and one mouth.

Mission Comes from our Common Life

The observer and the speaker are not lone individuals, but participants with others, sharing the wisdom, strength and folly of the whole Christian community. Personal as well as corporate response must be discerned and shared. As in the Celtic or Benedictine way, there is a personal journey and exploration, but it is carried out in a local community, sharing a common way of life, a vocation for all the baptised, to be God's people in their own place.

Therefore
Mission is rooted in the common life
of prayer
of learning
and of hospitality.

10

THE CHURCH AND THE ARTS

Robert Cooper

If your ministry is one of leading worship and teaching, you cannot afford to ignore the arts. For one thing, you would discount the experience of all the people who find creative activities valuable. For another, you would end up with a lop-sided theology in which words and concepts are given excessive value. As Neil Smith of the Community of Christ the King has written: 'The arts are about revelation and are therefore a profound pathway to engagement with spiritual truth'.[1]

This chapter gives some pointers towards the practical importance of creative activities. It then offers some reflection on the theological significance of the arts.

Using Creative Activities
Creativity and learning

The culture of the Church is dominated by words. The sermon remains its basic teaching method. Yet it is now recognised that 'I talk – you listen' is the least effective way of enabling people to learn. In today's world, television and computer screens are increasingly replacing the verbal with the visual. Much of the Church's approach, therefore, is at odds with a culture in which other forms of education emphasise opportunities for participating and doing.

It may seem obvious to say that different people learn in different ways. Yet Churches often fail to offer a variety of learning strategies. Without participative activities as an essential ingredient in a programme of Christian education, some people are denied their most fulfilling way to come to God and for God to come to them.

Participative activity can empower those who feel 'disabled' by words and concepts. They find creative activity – perhaps involving drama or making something – inviting, because it means joining in and taking part. It also integrates action and reflection, mind and body, thought and intuition, whereas purely conceptual learning (such as listening to a sermon) does not.

Those whose preferred learning mode is conceptual can also learn in this way, even though they may find it demanding. All human beings have a left and a right side to the brain. Both need to be valued and used. Faced with a practical activity, conceptualisers can be reluctant to get involved. They are often used to appearing as society's most competent people. They can therefore feel threatened by activities which they sense (consciously or subconsciously) will expose some weakness. In particular, creative activity of most kinds leads into the world of experience. Instead of merely talking about something like the fragility of life, it is felt. Such fears need sensitive handling. However, they offer an opportunity for healing and for growth in a neglected area of the self.

A licensed Reader, perhaps selected precisely for skill with words, knows, nevertheless, that words are not always necessary for spiritual discovery or an encounter with God. Children and many adults prefer a more concrete approach, but may be uncertain how to respond. Reflecting on the arts or using creative activities offers one way forward.

Creativity and worship

Worship, in whatever tradition, uses symbols. The best symbols do not require explaining – they speak to a deeper level within us. Witness the way in which all sorts of people find help through lighting a candle. But Old Testament warnings against idols have left their mark. They leave some Christians mistrustful of images intended as aids to worship, such as icons or statues. And when the Word is also central to worship, as in the Protestant tradition, symbol and action are downgraded. Seldom, for example, is baptism allowed to speak for itself, without verbal explanation. This may be partially justified because the Church and the world no longer share a symbolic language. But it is also the result of liturgy 'done' without conviction. When properly 'performed' with trust in the power of symbols to speak for themselves, they can.

The idea of liturgy as 'performance' – theatrical – is not new. But it should suggest to those responsible for it that there are things they can learn from performance artists through observation and personal contact. So, look for opportunities to involve performers in imaginative liturgy – they can encourage and help the Church in the challenging task of creating worship which involves action as much as words.

Faith and the arts – a shared exploration

In looking for those from any sphere of the arts who will support our work, we must not limit ourselves to practising Christians. The artist and the person of faith are on a similar journey. The common ground we share is a commitment to celebrate and explore the heights and depths of human existence, and identify the barriers that need to be removed if people are to grow towards the full humanity which the Christian believes is God's will for all (John 10:10). This shared quest engages with the deep realities of life.

Endless opportunities – not just worship – exist for involving arts practitioners in this common exploration. Over the centuries artists have served the Church. Works of art, such as stained glass and paintings, have illustrated its teachings. Composers have set its central texts to music. But the contribution of the artist goes far beyond this. More importantly, their work reflects something of the mystery of God and enhances worship through the creation of mood.

But do not presume from this that works of art are valuable merely as visual or aural aids. The value of art does not lie primarily in 'illustrating' Christian teaching. It is not only sacred art or Christian artists who can enlighten. Artists who are sympathetic to spiritual concerns, but not necessarily believers, are less bound by preconceptions. They are better able to exercise the artist's gift of seeing familiar things with fresh insight.

So, for example, if you're planning to use a painting rather than words as a focus for meditation, it does not have to be a religious one. A totally secular painting, such as Münch's *The Scream,* may achieve more, than perhaps, one of the crucifixion. This painting speaks starkly about human suffering and alienation. In its light, the crucified Christ's cry of abandonment can be seen as part of God's response to the universal human experience of suffering. And because the painting comes from a less familiar context its message is stronger.

So look for ways to encourage the Church to offer hospitality to performers and to artworkers. Living with an artist's vision and having the chance to ask questions about the creative process can be an illuminating experience, both in the narrow sphere of the religious and the broader sphere of the human, which is shared territory.

Some Theological Reflections

Much of what has been touched upon so far has significant theological implications. Six brief thoughts are offered below to encourage further reflection.

Creativity offers insight into God

Through the first chapter of Genesis runs the refrain 'Let there be...'. The desire and the will to 'let there be...' lies behind all creativity. It is therefore a unique means of gaining a deeper understanding of God's activity. Self-giving love is how W. H. Vanstone characterises this activity in his book *Love's Endeavour, Love's Expense* (SCM, 1977). The whole book is worth reading, but pages 30-35 offer a particularly valuable insight. Vanstone describes how two boys make a model of an area around a waterfall, using stones, twigs, plaster and paint. He writes about their initial reluctance, but growing absorption. As the model progresses, he notes the intensity of their discussions when faced by choices which become limited by earlier decisions. The boys find some materials 'right', but others 'difficult'. They are surprised by the use to which apparently unattractive materials can be put and the unexpected value they can assume. They discover how to respond when something goes wrong. Above all, Vanstone is moved by the boys' increasing care as the model takes shape and how they watch and wait more, allowing the model to teach them the next move. They begin to allow the model a certain power over them.

With immense sensitivity, Vanstone uses this story to express his understanding of God's relationship with creation. What it also offers is a paradigm of how the eyes of our understanding can be enlightened through a creative activity such as this. In particular, Vanstone emphasises how any creative work necessitates struggle and risk because at no point is it possible to be entirely certain of the final result. Such things speak of God's nature and action. They also speak of what it means to become fully human, made in the image of God.

Beauty matters

Part of what the arts have to offer is a sense of beauty. Bishop Leonard Wilson was interned and tortured during the Second World War. Writing later he said, 'There was a tiny window at the back of the cell, and through the bars I could hear the song of the golden oriole. I could see the glowing red flame of the forest tree, and something of God's indestructible beauty was communicated to my tortured mind.' Neil Smith writes, 'The search for beauty is universal; it is a spiritual searching for the creative force which sustains all things.' Creative activity and experience are essential to Christian growth, because they involve people with beauty in a way that is fundamental to their becoming fully human.

Creativity and spirituality

Creativity can stimulate personal reflection and prayer. This is because the essence of both prayer and creativity is paying attention. Activities like drawing or writing demand close observation. Respect for materials is essential to sculpture and the crafts. Listening deeply is fundamental, not only to the creation of music, but to its performance. But the attention required by creativity is not simply an illuminating parallel to prayer – it can be prayer in itself. The true artist not only looks, but sees – and this deep looking is a spiritual activity.

Such things take time. But in a Western world obsessed with business, we need to learn to 'waste' time. A work of art cannot proceed without a standing back for silence and reflection. Let art teach us that a life cannot be made by scurrying around.

Creative activity is an experience of the body of Christ

Creativity can be a solitary experience. But it can also offer an experience of the truth that human fulfilment lies in interdependence with others. Creativity is about nourishing and cherishing gifts. It is about celebrating variety. As part of a weekend on 'Art and Wholeness' a group was invited to sit together to draw a great cedar tree. Each person drew a section in their own style. They had, however, to be in continual consultation with their neighbours to ensure that the sections married up. Joined together, the drawings were an expression of diversity within unity. Within the single tree, the uniqueness of each contribution was preserved. What St Paul says about the body of Christ (1 Corinthians 12) had been understood through experience.

Creative activity is also particularly effective in enabling collaboration between adults and children. Here they can work together, sometimes as equals, sometimes with the adults leading, sometimes with the children leading. In a similar way, when learning is a participative activity, understanding comes to be seen as residing in the group, rather than in an individual expert. Besides this, when we use creative activities we will find ourselves calling on people who might not normally be expected to take on a leadership or teaching role. We will therefore find ourselves affirming a wide variety of gifts in God's service and the value of individuals in general.

Creativity is healthily subversive

Frequently in our society, people are valued more for what they do than for who they are. The so-called Protestant Work Ethic is partly to blame, with its fear of 'idle hands'. But so too are the economic values which dominate current thought. The highly-paid are highly-valued, because consumers are the diet of the insatiable economic dragon. The impact of both these things on those without paid employment or women in the home, for example, is devastating.

The Church should be foremost amongst those saying that human meaning and value are not defined by productivity. The justification for this is worship. Worship is the highest human calling. It is also a supremely 'unproductive' activity! Creativity is often unproductive in precisely the same way. Clearly, it can be a means of making a living. However, even then, the creative urge often remains rooted in a personal joy and fulfilment completely at odds with both the work ethic and economic productivity. As such, it subverts our present system of values, by reminding us to let go and to play. It is tempting to wonder if some of this may have been in Jesus' mind when he said, 'Whoever does not receive the kingdom of God like a child shall not enter it' (Luke 18:17). Children do not need to be taught to play or to wonder. In his book *Original Blessing* (Bear and Co., 1983) Matthew Fox quotes the medieval theologian Meister Eckhart who writes about this childlike need 'to live without a why, to work without a why, to love without a why'. Fox comments that perhaps 'the time has come to play with God more than to pray to God and in our play true prayer will emerge'. Let the arts and creative activities offer you ways in which to explore this exciting possibility.

The arts encourage open-ended exploration

The 'journey of faith' has become a common image. It is

nonetheless valuable for that. It is an image which implies new horizons and unexpected possibilities. Using the arts and creative activities supports this approach. Science places value on certainty and proof. The arts encourage struggle, risk and uncertainty. Such things make for growth.

The arts offer those making the journey of faith a picture of what they are doing with their lives. They speak of 'making something of ourselves'. We can picture that something as a poem, a dance, a symphony – 'something beautiful for God'. To quote Matthew Fox again, 'The most beautiful thing that the potter creates is... the potter'.

But creative activities can touch our relationships as well as ourselves. A curate tells of a drama exercise in which he had to wrestle with the bishop who ordained him. 'Till then I had felt the bishop to be a rather aloof figure. But now I found myself "laying hands" on the man who had "laid hands" on me and my experience of the relationship became quite different. Afterwards, I could never think of him in quite the same way again. It was partly because he gave himself generously to the exercise and did not hide behind his role and authority. It was also simply because I touched him. As a result he became a person of flesh and blood, someone I could relate to as a normal human being'. Sometimes, when words fail, a creative, participative experience proves to be a breakthrough.

NOTES

1. From an unpublished paper for the Arts and Recreation Chaplaincy of the North East.
2. Ibid.

ENEMY OF APATHY

She sits like a bird, brooding on the waters,
hovering on the chaos of the world's first day;
she sighs and she signs, mothering creation,
waiting to give birth to all the Word will say.
She wings over earth, resting where she wishes,
lighting close at hand or soaring through the skies;
she nests in the womb, welcoming each wonder,
nourishing potential hidden to our eyes.

She dances in fire, startling her spectators,
waking tongues of ecstasy where dumbness reigned;
she weans and inspires all whose hearts are open,
nor can she be captured, silenced or restrained.

For she is the Spirit, one with God in essence,
gifted by the Saviour in eternal love;
she is the key opening the scriptures,
enemy of apathy and heavenly dove.

From *Enemy of Apathy*, vol 2,
John Bell and Graham Maule, 1988.

PART FIVE
A VISION OF THE FUTURE

11

THE END OF THE BIBLE AND A VISION OF THE FUTURE
A STUDY IN THE BOOK OF REVELATION

David Jenkins

A lightly edited Bible Study from the Central Readers' Council National Conference, at the College of St Hild and St Bede, Durham University.

I am going to range quite widely through the Book of Revelation, not least because I am getting increasingly fed up with people who think that you can understand the Bible by sticking to snippets, or even worse, to verses. So there is a sense in which I am on the spiritual warpath.

Let me explain quickly my reasons for choosing the Book of Revelation. I chose it because of the context of *Vision 2000*. That is to say, how should we look forward to the mission and ministry of the Church in the new millennium? And therefore the question arises: How are we to build a sound spiritual and theological base for this? In other words, how should we seek to understand God? (because that is what theology is about). And then, how can our understanding of God be grown into, and developed out of, our life, work and ministry? (and that is spirituality). In this Benedictine context we pick up a phrase which Anselm (the great Benedictine Abbot of Beck and Archbishop of Canterbury) himself took from Augustine: *fides quaerens intellectum* – 'faith seeking understanding'. That comprehends more than just using the intellect; it is a question of going into the depths of relying on the assurance of faith to take risks, to gain perspectives; how to begin and progress further and further in (if I may so put it) seeing and feeling things in relation to God. The editors have asked us to consider that Durham provides us with a possible set of resources, experience and tradition for this practical and down-to-earth building up of theology and spirituality into the next millennium.

The editors ask us to consider 'when Celtic spirituality meets Benedictine Rule'. Here I would just like to slip in evidence that this is very much part of my own pilgrimage. I have the Rule of Benedict, which was presented to me in Durham Cathedral at my enthronement, and a specially made copy (though slightly adapted) of the cross of St Cuthbert which was commissioned by my wife for my episcopate. You see, therefore, that the matter is intensely personal to me. Which, of course, is what all spirituality has to be. (That is not the same as making it ultra-individualistic, by the way – that is the modern heresy, of course.)

I gather that this meeting of Celtic spirituality and Benedictine Rule, being reflected in the history of Durham and still so much part of the history of the North East, has been taken as demonstrating that there are two things which should interact. Benedictine Rule – the framework and the work of prayer. The *Opus Dei* is the work of prayer in a framework, in a community – interacting with a Celtic spirituality which is taken to be, in some ways, more open and more free-ranging. (You never knew when Cuthbert would wander off, and where he would turn up next – and even, I think, what he would say.) So the Celtic spirituality contributed a more free-ranging monasticism (not so highly organised as the Benedictine), a more subordinate episcopacy (not dressed up in purple) and a missionary strategy which was open, flexible, mobile; and all this in a context of what some people call 'nature-mysticism'. You know, openness – sheer openness to the sky and the living creatures and the context.

The editors hinted that we in the Church of England might be getting a bit too set on ordering, managing, central-aim setting and cost accounting, to the detriment of the free-ranging depth and exploration and experimental freedom of the Spirit.

Reflecting on all this made me think, of course, of the

millennium, and of the fact that nobody knows quite what to put in the Millennium Dome, and in particular, that nobody wants to sponsor a Dome exhibition on the spirit and all that. Frankly, I don't blame them. For one reason, if you are so vague about the spirit, it might as well be left out; for another, the spirit must be found everywhere else. So I am not particularly worried about this, but it raises a good question. It was this that made me think of the Book of Revelation. For it is the book which comes at the end of the Bible and contains a particular vision of the End. As part of our spiritual quest, I want to consider whether the book is in any way a suitable book to be the end of the Bible – personally, I think it is not; precisely because, in one sense, the Bible does not have an End. But I shall come to that.

Revelation does say that God is about everything and he is going somewhere. This is the real issue of AD 2000– whether it is more than a conventional date. Originally, of course, this appellation meant that everything is to be dated against what has been revealed in Jesus. So everything before Jesus is leading up to Jesus; and everything from Jesus is going towards God's future. So AD 2000 actually means, 'you are in a process going from Creation to fulfilment' (I do not think that computers are aware of that), and all is to be understood in Christ, under God and through the Spirit – hence, spirituality. God is about everything in time, space and eternity – or (and this, I believe, is the basic challenge) he/she/it does not exist. I think it is important to be clear about that. Except that one must not use the word 'existence' for philosophical reasons. That is to say, 'either God is and is about everything or there is no God' – all in one phrase, you see? It is not a question of existence; it is a question of what everything is about.

This is the third millennium challenge to the religions. The religions seem to spend their time fussing about who is more right than someone else, how to enforce rather doubtful moralities, how to convert and so on. Neuroses about women. Neurosis squared about sex. And tendencies to quote the Bible as long as you leave out that half of the verse which says, 'if you do that you will be killed'. It is well to laugh – because sin – by God's great Grace – will not have dominion over us, even in the Church. But it is damnably serious, this trivialising of religion and God. Have we Christians so learned Christ?

So, I thought, look at the last book of the Bible, the Apocalypse of the End. *Apocalypsos*, as you know, means 'unveiling'. The unveiling as given in St John is so hellishly apocalyptic that that is what apocalypse has come to mean; but it did not start out by meaning that. It means what it is used, or chosen, to mean – like Humpty Dumpty said. The Apocalypse of the End.

Obviously, as we examine a selection of texts, we begin at the beginning. On the first page of the Book of Revelation we find a reference to a person, some reference to a location, and some evidence about a 'genre' (what sort of thing is going on?). I do not intend to pursue what is called the Christology of Christ or Jesus in the Book of Revelation. It is really very confused. But that does not matter here.

> The apocalypse of Jesus Christ, which God gave Jesus to show his servants what must soon take place. He made it known by sending his angel or messenger to his servant John

> – who testifies to everything that he saw.

The only other clue about John comes in verse 9:

> I, John, your brother and companion in the suffering and kingdom and patient endurance that are ours in Jesus, was on the island of Patmos because of the word of God and the testimony of Jesus.

It so happens that I have visited the island of Patmos a number of times and that I have also been to the sites of four of the seven churches. Because of this, when I go as a lecturer on a classical cruise, I often try to give people the feel of what was there before. This has helped me to appreciate just how down-to-earth the letters to the seven churches are. There is another experience I had at Patmos. Because of me, and others like me, we are no longer allowed to lecture on the steps on the way down to the chapel where St John is supposed to have leant (there is a hole for his elbow, you understand) and where he is said to have written this text. Because we have thought it necessary to say, first, that it is almost certain that the John of the Revelation is not John the Evangelist. The matters are: a) Greek style; b) theological style. It is very, very difficult to imagine what are almost the crudities of the Greek, and even worse the crudities of the middle chapters, being written by the Evangelist, St John. There is the further reference, in the really exciting bit about the New Jerusalem, that 'the walls of the city have twelve frameworks and on them were the names of the twelve apostles of the Lamb'. That suggests an author who was distanced from all this. So we do not know who 'John' is.

Patmos, as a matter of fact, never appears again in records until about AD 1000 when a rich Greek persuaded the emperor to let him found a monastery there. The point, which is encapsulated for me in my personal experience, is that, now that it has become The Tradition that the author of the Fourth Gospel wrote the Book of Revelation in this specific cave, if you try to say anything to the contrary, you are taken to be destroying tradition, attacking faith itself and are thrust out with anger. If we are going to be faithful witnesses into the twenty-first century we have got to realise that *this will not do.*

The emergence of traditions – even the 'finding of the True Cross' had its origins in the fourth century – and then making them the basis of faith, is sheer superstition, idolatry and ignorance. And this has to be said to the Greek Orthodox Church in private when required. It cannot stand up to what it means to preach the gospel in Nigeria when the dominating power is Shell Inc. I cannot be too clear about this. My passion arises out of my evangelicalistic desire, which has become clear to me, that, if I have anything to witness to, now I am in my eighth decade, it is that this nonsense, this faithlessness, this superstition must cease. It must, if we want to share the glory of the Word of God, who is the crucified Jesus, who comes to us in the Spirit.

The location of the seven churches is clear enough: Ephesus, Smyrna, Pergamum and Sardis are all on the Western coast of Asia Minor; but Thyatira, Philadelphia and Laodicea are found a little inland. If you go to a site, for instance Sardis, its remains go back to before Jesus; there is a most splendid Jewish synagogue. It probably dates from the early third century AD, so it is not quite contemporary with these readings, but it is a strong reminder that when you get the Jews popping up, as you do in the messages, there was a flourishing culture going on. We are not dealing with special biblical examples, but with poor struggling people in an utterly confused Middle East trying to make sense of what is happening to them. They must not be over-sanctified, or made mythical. They are real.

From the physical location we move on to the location in the genre – what type?

> I turned around to see the voice that was speaking to me. And when I turned I saw seven golden lamp-stands and among the lamp-stands was someone like a son of man.

That is the sign of what the genre is. This text is like the Book of Daniel. In Daniel 7:13 you even get the fiery hair and all the rest of it. This is an attempt by the author of Revelation – a vivid, a literally fantastic attempt, containing clues which relate to the history contemporary at the time of writing – to produce this apocalyptic literature. This is the literature which people have come to take (though not so much nowadays as in the past) as evidence of God's programme. But of course it is not an evidence of God's programme. It is an assurance about God's purpose and persistence. And any attempt to read out a programme as to how the world will go, either from the Book of Daniel or from the Book of Revelation, is to fly in the face of the facts. This is partly demonstrated by the fact that everybody reinterprets these texts every time. It comes down in a humorous way to the fact that even the chap who dated the birth of Jesus – and on whose calculations we base our AD 2000 – has got it wrong. So the mercy is that, if the apocalypse is going to occur in the year 2000, it happened five years ago.

It is very important to laugh. Because there will be so much solemn prophecy and pomposity and piffle trotted out at the so-called millennium. It is a disgrace to God that this sort of thing is taken seriously. Do you really think that God is so small-minded that he has an almanac, which he invented in the year dot, and always sticks to it? If he does, then he is the very devil. I mean, look what actually happens. God takes many, many, many more risks than that. I do not believe he has a 'plan'; he has a purpose. He perseveres in his purpose. And not even all the stuff that is in the Book of Revelation puts him off. Indeed, not all the things that you and I do in the Church put him off, either (just in case you feel too detached). The point is: '*Do not be afraid, I am the first and the last. The beginning and the End*' – this is what it is all about!

> I am the living one. I was dead (the Resurrection) and behold I am alive forever and ever, and I hold the keys of death and Hades.

That is what you have to discover in every circumstance. That is what the Book of Revelation is about. So we get this down-to-earth realism in the Letters to the Seven Churches, which we find in chapters 2 and 3. I shall just pick out a bit from each. For example, we start with Ephesus:

But you have this in your favour. You hate the practices of the Nicolaitons which I also hate.

Sounds like General Synod, doesn't it? 'Le plus ça change, le plus c'est la même chose.' General neurosis about what is truth, and so you hate somebody instead of trying to investigate it. Amazing, really. Quite encouraging in another way. It is rather like going back to Genesis 3. God has had problems with us from the beginning and he never gives up. There is a funny side to it, but the message to the church in Smyrna is the unfunny side of it.

I tell you, the Devil will put some of you in prison to test you. And you will suffer persecution for ten days. Be faithful. Even to the point of death, and I will give you the crown of life.

This is serious, even if, at times, you do better to laugh than to weep. That is reinforced in the church at Pergamum. The thirteenth verse of the message to the church of Pergamum:

You did not renounce your faith in me, even in the days of Antipas, my faithful witness, who was put to death in your city, where Satan lives.

You see how serious this is? Some friend of ours has been killed for this. It is important to grasp this fully when you come to some of the hate, fear, and rejoicing at murder which comes later in the Book. People were so frightened. People felt so helpless. Nothing seemed to happen. The powers-that-be were wholly against them. We have got to take the full nature of what enters into our hearts and minds in the situations we come into. People do well to be upset when they are uncertain – even if spirituality requires uncertainty. How do we marshall the pastoralia, the faith and the courage to see people through the bottom of their experiences into this hopefulness?

Then – see the bad temper, again, in the church in Thyatira. This gets tough.

> Nevertheless, I have this against you. You tolerate that woman Jezebel who calls herself a prophetess. By her teachings she misleads my servants into sexual immorality and the eating of food sacrificed to idols. I have given her time to repent of her immorality, but she is unwilling. So I will cast her on a bed of suffering and I will make those who commit adultery with her suffer immensely unless they repent of her ways. I will strike her children dead.

That is the way to clear nonsense like homosexuality and bestiality out of the Church, eh? – Or is it? You can understand why people might have got that angry, but is that learning Christ? It is very human. It is very down-to-earth.

Look how it continues in the message to Thyatira. He quotes from a Psalm:

> He will rule them with an iron sceptre. He will dash them to pieces like pottery.

Now you are going to get about ten chapters of dashing things to pieces. Is this to be taken literally? Supposing that was read in church. Would you get up tamely and say: 'This is the Word of the Lord. Thanks be to God'? I think our liturgicologists are getting a bit too precious. They ought to be a bit tougher. One of the alternative revisions to be used at will should be: 'Oh no it isn't!' – providing you will take responsibility for it.

So it goes on. The angel of the church in Sardis, my goodness!

> I know your deeds. You have a reputation of being alive, but you are dead. Wake up! Strengthen what remains and is about to die. But I have not found your deeds complete in the sight of my God.

The warning that we always require – in the middle of things people just settle down to a routine and we need waking up. And of course, last of all, there is the really famous extract from the letter to Laodicea about people having to be spat out because they are neither hot nor cold. I remember a person once instructing me in the confessional, saying he had people who came and he felt like saying to them: 'Oh do go away and commit a real sin. Then you can really repent.' This too has its funny side. It has all been the same over and over again. Then you have the famous bit at the end of the message to the Laodiceans:

> Here I am. I stand at the door and knock. If anyone hears my voice, and opens the door, I will come in and eat with him and he with me.

Now that can be rather Holman Hunt-ised and turned into a rather wet figure trying to get in. If you read the rest of the Book, of course, it shows that if you let Jesus in, there may be hell to pay – in one sense. Because it is a real wrestle with this real, down-to-earthness; with what is going on around you which can be completely out of your control. So I find it very, very human indeed. That is what I find encouraging. For that is clearly what our God, in Christ, through the Spirit, copes with. It is not about coping with things we idealise or fantasise about. That is how, I think, you come through the Throne in Heaven in chapter 4 (of course, the Throne in Heaven raises the question: Who is in charge, and how?), to this remarkable vision in chapter 5, or the Lamb on the Throne. This passage needs a lot of exposition, but I am just making one point here.

Then there is this business of being directed towards the Throne of God in Heaven,

> And then I saw a Lamb, looking as if it had been slain, standing in the centre of the Throne.

This is obviously the crucified Christ ruling the world. In the middle of all this, and you are going to get devastating warfare – the Throne is occupied by the Lamb. Read the hymn of praise at the end of chapter 5.

> Worthy is the lamb who was slain to receive power and wealth and wisdom and strength, and honour, and praise. And then I heard every creature in Heaven and on earth, and under the earth, and on the sea and all that is in them, singing. To him who sits on the Throne and to the Lamb be praise and honour and glory and power forever and ever.

That is where true power, true praise, true promise are enthroned. In the purposes of God, in him who was slain. If you want to know about power, you have to think about the Cross. It is very difficult, and desperately difficult to apply. It is beautifully summed up in my favourite theologian, whom I am always quoting, the deceased, atheist Jew, Mel Calman. Calman was a cartoonist who drew 'his God', this little man in a nightshirt with a beard. And he had his God going to sleep on a cloud. And he can't get to sleep because of the noise of strife rising up from the earth below. And he leans over his cloud with a cross face and the caption reads: 'Love one another – or I'll come down and bash you!' Now again, isn't that a profound piece of theology? Or at any rate, an invitation. For, you see, God didn't. He did not come down and bash us. And if he is going to judge, how will he? If we have to judge, *en route*, how should we behave? That is the real question. I think that the picture of the Lamb on the Throne is very, very remarkable in the midst of all this other stuff that we are going to come to.

You should read through from chapter 6 to chapter 19 and see all the horrors, and the beasts, and the seven trumpets and the seven plagues and the seven this-es and thats, and all the rejoicing in these horrors. Consider two symptomatic verses out of all the pathological section in the middle. Firstly, from the last verse of chapter 13:

This calls for wisdom. If anyone has insight, let him calculate the number of the beast. For it is man's number. His number is 666.

That has been the subject of much speculation, and it is now known to be the emergency number upside-down. And so on and so on! That should remind you of the way the genre is working. God has it all measured out, and if you can only interpret or break the code, then you will know what is going on.

Now, I believe that God is persevering and loving, and able to maintain his purpose through anything, but I do not believe for a moment that he is working it all out to a precise, preconceived plan. And you do not break the code. You suffer forwards with God. But all this is in the scriptures, you know.

Secondly, chapter 19. I take chapter 19 because it presents us with a problem. Verse 11, the rider on the white horse:

I saw Heaven standing open and there before me was a white horse, whose rider is called faithful and true. With justice he judges and makes war... . He has a name written on him that no-one but himself knows. He is dressed in a robe dipped in blood and his name is the word of God.

That is the name that is going to be given as 'King of Kings', 'Lord of Lords'. This picks up the earlier business of 'treading out the wrath of God in the vine press'; 'oceans of blood'. It ends up with the last paragraph:

Then I saw the beast and the kings of the earth, and their armies gathered together, and they are all destroyed.

Then the last verse of chapter 19 sees the rest of them killed 'with the sword that came out of the mouth of the rider on the horse'. (That is the Word of God.) 'And all the birds gorged themselves on their flesh.' This is the way God is going to bring things to an End?

Well – how pathological can you get? Then there is a giddy joke of a postscript. That is what leads to the thousand years from which we draw the phrase 'Millennium'. No wonder we do not know what the millennium is about. It was an apocalyptic picture about saying there is a period of time and then a period. We haven't taken our Bible studies seriously, I think, and simply used the language.

So we move, finally, to the last chapter, chapter 21.

> Then I saw a new heaven and a new earth. For the first Heaven and the first earth has passed away, and there was no longer any sea. (You can tell that they came from the inland of the Middle East, can't you?) I saw the holy city, the new Jerusalem, coming down out of heaven, prepared as a bride, beautifully dressed for her husband. And I heard a loud voice from the throne, saying, 'now the dwelling of God is with men'. And he will live with them. They shall be his people, and God himself will be with them, and be their God. He will wipe away every tear from their eyes. There will be no more death or mourning, or crying or pain. For the old order of things has passed away. He who was seated on the throne said: I am making everything new. Then he said, for these words are trustworthy and true.

This amazing vision arising out of and after all that pathology. 'I am making all things new' – reminding us of all sorts of things, especially through the New Testament; you know, that lovely verse in 2 Corinthians 5:17: 'If anyone is in Christ there is a new creation.' Old things have gone. 'Look! Newness is there!' (In Greek the verb is in the perfect tense – 'Look! There's newness!') Next time you hold a Parochial Church Council meeting think of that in the middle!

Again in 2 Peter 3:13:

> But in keeping with his promises we are looking forward to
> a new heaven and a new earth. The home of righteousness,
> justice, peace.

And in Hebrews 13:14:

> For here we do not have an abiding city, but we are looking
> for the city that is to come.

Next time there is a row about changing the liturgy, think of
that. (Not that I am in favour of changing the liturgy now that I
am seventy-three. It annoys me no end. But that is off the record.)
There is actually a pun in the Greek there, I think. The Greek
means 'We don't have an *abiding* city; we are looking for an
arriving one'. Abiding/arriving. We are on our way! Wake up! As
the angel has to say to the Church. This is the theme.

So we have here the spirituality, the theology, the reality of being
on the way to newness. And for this newness, look at 21:10-14:

> And he carried me away in the spirit to a mountain great and
> high, and showed me the holy city, Jerusalem, coming down
> out of Heaven from God. It shone with the glory of God. It
> had a great high wall with twelve gates, and with twelve angels
> at the gates. And on the gates were written the names of the
> twelve tribes of Israel. And there were three gates on the East,
> three on the North, three on the South and three on the West.
> And the wall of the city had twelve foundations, and on them
> were the names of the twelve apostles of the Lamb.

The final city has gathered up all the travails of Israel, all the
wanderings of the Church. And even more, if you go on to verse 22

But I did not see a temple in the city because the Lord God almighty and the Lamb are its temple. The city does not need the sun or the moon to shine on it, for the glory of God gives it light. And the Lamb is its lamp. The nations will walk by its light and the kings of the earth will bring their splendour into it.

Everything – you see – is being gathered up. As in the final passage I want to quote here: the opening verses of chapter 22.

Then the angel showed me the waters of the river of life, as clear as crystal, flowing from the throne of God and the Lamb down the middle of the great street of the city. And on each side of the river stood the tree of life bearing twelve crops of fruit, yielding their fruit every month, and its leaves and the leaves of the trees are for the healing of the nations.

All of a sudden, you see, it blossoms into a picture of the End as a universal vision despite, shall we say, the pathology and quarrelsomeness of the middle section, yet with the Lamb on the throne, and obviously very real people: just like us. Down-to-earth; being got down by things; taking it out of people and wondering where the hell we are going. What are we to make of it all? And what does it say to us?

It says something – does it not? – of immensely demanding and rewarding spirituality. Certainly it says that God is about everything. But the spiritual question we have to live with is: Is the way the Book of Revelation talks about it, is that the saving way; this saving catastrophe? We have to relate this to how we go into the next millennium (if the dating continues, or whether the dating is changed). God is going somewhere. Creation, love and judgment belong to the Alpha and the Omega: the whole alphabet of which history and eternity is spelt. All, as we believe, embodied in the Word, Jesus.

The final point for wrestling with you is contained 'in the Word Jesus' – but clearly not in words. To wrestle with this we need the spiritual discipline of the fellowship of belonging, of people who will help us to check up on ourselves; fellows who will keep us going when we falter; who will bring to us riches (from this tradition and that, this piece of learning and that – this piece of experience and that). The fellowship of the brothers and sisters in the discipline of pilgrimage. That was something the Benedictines tried to set up; something which is clearly for all. If we are to wrestle with the great depth of this vision and glory and mystery and love, in relation to all the mess and muddle and fear and death and torture – as well as all the happiness and jollity and celebration – that we are mixed up in, then surely we need to learn and develop a great spiritual openness. A spiritual openness to the newness which God is offering us as people on a pilgrimage to his heaven, Kingdom, City, End – his very self.

I think it worth noting here what I happened to discover, because I keep with my Rule of Benedict, a supplement of a Jesuit magazine called *The Way* which Father Don Columba Carey Elwes sent me from Ampleforth at the time of my Enthronement as Bishop of Durham. This is a supplement on the Benedictine life. On the second chapter of the Rule of Benedict on prayer, he comments thus: The point is, that whatever the details of his (Benedict's) Rule, prayer was central for Benedict and for his monks. Following tradition means development, adaptation and right interpretation.

Rooted in prayer, you see. Because prayer is the practice of the presence, or the waiting on the presence, or the hoping for the presence, or trying to be calm when the presence isn't there. 'Following tradition means development, adaptation and right interpretation. Fundamentalism kills tradition. It is for us to grasp and interpret the substance of the Rule, teaching within the context of our own time and conditions. Only in this way will we help those who follow to carry out a similar transposition for theirs.'

Fundamentalism kills tradition; we have to learn the transposition because we are pilgrims on the Way.

This ties up in my mind with one of the pictures I like best out of the Life of Cuthbert. The way in which he built his two cells with a wall around them, so that he would only see the sky. But remember, people came to the guest house and he was having dealings with people all the time. But he could retire simply to see the sky. And I have discovered, as I have been driven around the diocese of Durham during my episcopate, because of the roads that run along the crest of the land, and so on, – there are an amazing set of points where you can see 180 degrees of sky. And I can think that I dare share with Cuthbert a bit of the knowledge that that is the openness of God. It covers everything. It goes far beyond our sight. But it is there – or here among us.

That is why, amid all these uncertainty questions which are so necessary, we must be rooted in one another, in fellowship, in prayer and worship.

How shall we learn Christ for the twenty-first century? This is the challenge and this is the offer of Christian worship, discipleship and spirituality on the eve of the twenty-first century. Now, it doesn't matter about millennia. Together we are to receive the power and the presence of the Spirit: to encourage one another to look above; to look beyond but not around the corner; to look through the middle; to look beyond – and of course (this is one of the most important things about spirituality), to look within. 'Don't you know', says St Paul, 'that your body is the temple of the Holy Spirit?' I think we often panic by getting worried about that. How shall we get *there*, what will happen *then*? And the Lord says: 'Now shut up. Just look in for a moment. (He never says, 'shut up', as a matter of fact. That is how I address myself. He is far too polite.) This is what we have to help one another to do because we have been called into the people of God who know that God is greater than great (the sky), in his power and his presence and his promise of Love. We know, by things like 'the Lamb on the throne', that God is as he is in Jesus, and so is more loving than love – and at the same time more down-to-earth, more realistic, more involved, more capable of enduring than we are.

It must always be spiritually wrong to dodge any reality, you see, because God is even more real. I think that must be so.

Thirdly, there is the hope of going forward – not because of ourselves, but because of the Spirit within us; because of the Spirit which unites us together. And because, therefore, that we are not dependent on ourselves, we have to face (I think this may be a bit off-putting, but I think I must put it this way) the urgent need – out of our spirituality, our tradition, our worship and our fellowship – to rescue the Bible from being treated as 'scripture'.

'To rescue the Bible from being treated as scripture.' No matters of faith and witness, of morals and behaviour, of love and hope, can be settled by choosing biblical texts. You see, 'scripture' means 'that which is written'. And we have got tied down to 'that which is written', which, rather in the fashion of Humpty-Dumpty, we make mean what we want it to mean and pay it extra when it is especially important. (If it is a text on homosexuality, for instance; but we dodge the text on usury. That says nothing about usury or homosexuality, by the way; that is not what I am writing about at the moment.)

This way of going on will not do. If you choose a text – why do you choose that one? Secondly, who are you? How do you insist on a chosen interpretation and application? All sorts of problems come in. The arguments have to be worked out. Texts cannot settle anything. They may raise a proper question. The love of God and the future of God are far greater mysteries than that sort of thing.

I think we have to find the spiritual strength to move forward and say – quite clearly and simply – 'Of course the Bible is not the "Word" (capital W) of "God" (capital G)'. That is a manner of speaking which has grown up and been reinforced as people have become more and more literal-minded; as they have come to think that if you are to combat science you must be able to be as clear on your texts as science is on its 'scientific facts'. Of course, now we know that that does not work for science either. But people have lost their nerve. They like to say things like, 'we've got a theory as good as Newton' or 'a book as good as Einstein' or something. Well books and theories won't do. Not if you take them literally and text by text.

The Bible is a holy and a hallowed book, that contains and passes on the words of those who have come to believe that they have heard words from, or a Word about, the living God. The Bible is not the 'Word of God', it is full of the words of people who have felt inspired and obliged to speak words about God. You might allow, if you want be liturgical: 'This is the word of God via his servant Paul.' (Not always sound on women, Paul – for instance – you know what I mean. Or, whatever you like.) The Bible, therefore, is the precious gift of those who are preserving and passing on what they have, in their time and place, learnt and understood. Of course it is focused in the very particularity of Jesus Christ, which is why I think you do have to have two testaments and a rounding off of the Canon. But that does not stop the life of God, the life of Jesus, the life of the Spirit, the life of the Church – and, of course, the life of the world. Because God created the world. He may have trouble with it, but I do not believe that he has as yet written it off.

This is a vital and essential part of the ways in which God gives himself to us and reveals himself. He risks sharing – with us and through us – for his and our future. The gift of the Bible is treasure in earthly vessels. As you can certainly see if you take seriously the pathology of the middle of the Book of Revelation. When people are getting worked up about texts from Leviticus (do look in Numbers and Judges and Joshua and so on) and see how it was firmly believed that God instructed, when he found a couple in fornication, that they should be pinned to the bed and the ground with a spear! That is Numbers 25, as a matter of fact. I should not draw too much attention to it, because it is not a fit book for children, you understand! But just simply read the Bible realistically. Then you will never dare to say that it is made up of nothing but the Word of God!

I have just got so fed up now, because I think God is marvellous! I think Jesus is unbelievably wondrous! And I think that the Spirit helps me. And I think that people need it so! We are in this beautiful world – look at it! We could use its resources to cure so many of its ills. We have the technical means, the information systems, we have the productive means. With the right use, say, of our genetic expertise we could do so much if we could be trusted to be good stewards and responsible. Yet we will not do it! We misuse drugs; we trash and pollute the earth and so on. Sin is so tragic because it is falling so short of the amazing glory of God. We do not need to go round telling people that they are sinners. We want to show them the glory and then we can bow down in forgiveness and hope before the glory of God.

That is why I am so bothered about this misuse of the Bible. Assurance, now – this is the spiritual matter, this is the Benedictine matter, this is belonging to the following of St Cuthbert – assurance is not the same as certainty. Assurance is knowing through one another's presence and in one's heart about the presence and the possibility of God; and when you have forgotten it all, somebody comes along and helps you – and you are reassured. Or, when you can hardly do anything – when you get slightly older than me, for I am beginning to creak – but move your legs, and you can get to church and the glory of the Eucharist will speak. It certainly does to me. That is assurance. That is promise. That is enlargement – and that, I think, is what spirituality is about. And that is why we must seek fellowship in disciplines like that guided within the Benedictine Rule, in the openness we learn from St Cuthbert, in the following of Christ. We have this hope because of the power of God – Father, Son and Holy Spirit. Amen.

12

A CHANGING GOD OR A CHANGING PEOPLE?

John Bell

John Bell was invited to respond to the questions, 'What are the challenges to Christian spirituality posed by the Millennium?' and, 'What advice would you care to give to an established Church such as the Church of England for a spirituality for the twenty-first century?' We expressed our concern about the relationship between worship and action in the context of Christian Community. The following chapter is an edited transcript of a live interview between the editors and John Bell.

Establishment

I have been working in Sweden in 1998 where its Established Church is about to disestablish itself and go from being funded by the government, and therefore influenced by the government, to being completely on its own. I think there are some parallels with the Church of England, as there are with the Protestant Churches in Germany. One of the things that a State Church has to deal with is the extent to which its tradition, and particularly its clerical tradition, has become a burden which mitigates against an open, relevant and buoyant spirituality among the people. Where you have a long tradition of bishops and deans and canons and priests; where you have an ecclesiastical establishment that goes back for five or six hundred years, then for those who are insiders, who are ordained, this is comfortable baggage with which they can deal. But for those who are not ordained I think it is baggage which sometimes diminishes their enthusiasm for faith or indeed their access to God.

If one compares the Celtic Church of the past with even the Benedictine organisation, Celtic spirituality was a much more comprehensively catholic lay thing. It was not ordered by the monks or even the writing abbotts like Columba, Patrick and Cuthbert, but a good deal of it was left to lay people to develop their own spiritual expression. And so in Ireland, during the last century, and in Scotland there were those collections of poems in Scotland called *Carmina Gadelica*, which have been for many people resources for prayer. These were not handed down from the Canons of the Church (either legal or human canons!). These were just prayers that people felt that they could originate and pass on to their grandchildren from person to person. The faith of these people was something which did not rely on a heavy ecclesiastical establishment. If you were on the Island of Barra there was no reason to believe that you would always have access to a priest who would say Mass. So, for example, on the Island of Barra there was a baptism 'rite' where the midwife baptised the children. This was a perfectly good way of coping with baptism locally.

There is a whole category of prayers for beginning the day and ending the day which do not fall into the pattern of Catholic or Anglican Morning or Evening Prayer. This allowed the events of the day, which were personal to these people, to be offered to God. Now when we come into mainstream Catholicism, Anglicanism, and indeed Presbyterianism, then all that kind of need to create spiritual energy in people becomes supplanted by the desire of the monastery or the ecclesiastical establishment to have things work in a way which will be in keeping with monastic or ecclesiastical lifestyles and not necessarily that which will be suited to the rural or urban lifestyles of the majority of the people.

I think that at the end of the twentieth century when we look back, or look on that which we are taking with us into the future, so much of it is dictated by the whims of the ecclesiastical establishment and so little is geared towards the life of the people. I think that one of the correctives which the Celtic tradition offers us is to see the life of the people, the relationship to the land, the business of everyday work, the incarnation of Christ in the homes and in the area of activities of people, as equally, if not more important, than keeping some Church establishment ticking over.

Editors: When we look at the Carmina Gadelica, *it strikes us that the prayers seem to be steeped in what is basically very Orthodox theology. There seems to be an assumption of a huge tradition of knowledge feeding the daily lives and prayers of these people. Would a modern people even begin to have any of this tradition available to them?*

I think that one of the things that the Celts did in the past was to educate the laity theologically. It is just astounding (I do not say this with any kind of nationalistic or xenophobic genes in my being), but people in the Western Isles were theologically very literate because they reflected on the purposes of God in creation. To some extent, if you go further back, when your tools for theological formation were high-standing crosses and illuminated manuscripts, then you taught the basics. And the basics you taught were God the creator of the world, Christ incarnate and the Spirit that helps sustain the whole of creation. For these people, God is concerned about health and healing, and about our relationship to the Other on which we depend. This is taught, not from pouring over Second Chronicles or doing an exegesis on Romans chapter 12. Their spirituality would be founded on the basic stories of the faith from the creation of the world up to redemption in Christ. This is a fundamental simplicity rather than naïveté.

We also have a great naïveté, but it masquerades as sophistication at the end of the twentieth century. Our great naïveté is that everybody should understand the Bible. Nobody has understood the Bible since the beginning of time. The Celtic people who have given us these orthodox nuggets of devotion and insight possibly would never have known the letter to Philemon; who perhaps had never poured over all these gruesome stories about judges; who had not been *au fait* with the intricacies of Levitical Law. However, they did know a basic canon of scriptural truth, which they were then charged to incorporate into the way they lived their lives.

I have to ask today what is the basic canon of scriptural truth which people have and which enables them to live their lives more astutely or more openly before God. We have a dichotomy, we have a great division, a dualism between the life of the Church, which has its own vocabulary, ceremonies and form of address, and the life of the world of computers, industry, shopping, commerce and trade, which at the moment is not suffused with the jargon of faith. You do not find this dichotomy in the Bible. The Psalms are highly secular poems. In the Psalms people weep. Their pillows are soaked with tears; folk are gossiped about; they feel bad about it and they are enraged because of the hooligans who want to destroy them. All of that seems to me to be in keeping with what people experience in the contemporary world. Yet, there has always been a barrier erected by the Church, which says, 'In order to appreciate the force of scripture, in order to let this psalm permeate your being, the Church has to interpret to you what it means.'

Now all my experience in working with people on the fringes of the Church is, that, when you make the connection between the raw life of secular humanity and the whole range of emotional expression, then the Book of Psalms immediately connects. We (the Iona Community) have done this with adults, and with people who are outside of the usual 'communities of faith' and with school-children. We want to remove the all-pervading clericalism, which is part and parcel of the Church's witness, and teach them to see the scripture and to feel for God in a much more direct fashion; and then trust them to make the connections. Sometimes people get it wrong. The Celts did not always get it right, but at least these lay people felt, and the Monks had allowed them to believe this, that God was for them and that God was one of them. When the women sang their naïve lullabies to Jesus, as if Jesus were lying in their arms, they were focusing on personal prayer to Christ in a much more meaningful and direct way than people today, who feel they have to go through the intercessory medium of spiritual 'Delia Smiths'.

When we look at how we try to get people to pray today, we find that we show them people like Teresa of Avila and Thomas Merton, with his multi-storey mountain. These people are extraordinary people. They did not lead lives in which they had to change nappies, or make soup, or deal with a thousand demands on their time. And yet, these classical writers are the grand models that we set up as being worthy of emulation by people who do not live in monasteries, who do not live their life according to the Hours of Prayer, and who do not get up at four o'clock in the morning. They are maybe going to bed at four o'clock in the morning!

So often, this is the medium through which devotion is imparted to people who live life in a totally secular society. We have to get away from this, and to some extent from the ecclesiastical establishment, an establishment which has to devolve itself of the power of interposing between the relationship between God and the people, in order that that relationship may be more honest. You know, I say this as a cleric, somebody who is ordained, one who believes that he was called by God to be a minister of the Church. I know how tempted I am to allow my ordained status and experience to be the measure of how other people should live.

Recently, when I was working with curates and probationers for the ministry, all their talk was about what they had learned at theological college and who they had met. And I thought, 'People are not interested in who you met, in what books you read, or in which theologians you sat under.' If they are interested in anything, it is whether God means anything to them. All your illustrations should not be, 'Well, when I was a curate', or 'When I was an ordinand', or, 'The first day I went into theological college.' It sounds as if you are saying that 'If you have not done what I have done, you cannot possibly be intimate with the Almighty.'

This is just a symbol, perhaps, an emblem, of a bigger malaise of all the established Churches. How do we have decent order in the Church and how do you have a paid ministry in the Church, and yet enable the Church to be the vehicle by which the piety of lay people is seen as of supreme worth and is encouraged? I see this as a fundamental challenge.

Editors: Sometimes when we look at various attempts that are made to write modern hymns or to tell modern parables it all turns out to be a bit contrived. Have you any advice as to how we enable a genuine expression of a true spirituality which relates to computers and blocks of flats? We can remember one dreadful hymn that refers to 'council flats'.

Yes, I see this, it questions the ability of contemporary language to reflect life in prayer, encapsulate it in song and offer it to God. Take a kitchen. A kitchen is a reality for 75 or 80 per cent of the British public. People spend their time in kitchens. Jesus spent a lot of time in kitchens because of the type of houses he visited. But try putting kitchen into a hymn. It does not work, partly because there is a musical standard, a kind of hymn sound, a diapason organ sound, which we associate with religious songs and that cannot deal with 'kitchen'. The tunes to 'Abide with Me' and 'Praise My Soul the King of Heaven' cannot deal with the word 'kitchen', yet 'kitchen' is the reality for people.

This to some extent shows how much eighteenth- and nineteenth-century hymnody has dominated the religious imagination. In the nineteenth century one of the social realities for people was child mortality, with a high rate of perinatal death, caused by a mixture of malnutrition, bad housing, bad pre- and post-natal care, and industrial accidents with children. Hymn writers wrote scores of hymns to deal with that reality. For example 'There is a Friend for little children above the bright blue sky... There is a rest for little children above the bright blue sky... There is a home for little children above the bright blue sky... There is a crown for little children above the bright blue sky... There is a song for little children above the bright blue sky... There is a robe for little children above the bright blue sky'. Even in the famous Christmas carol, 'Once in Royal David's City', we find the verse:

And our eyes at last shall see him,
through his own redeeming love
for that child so dear and gentle
is our Lord in heaven above:
and he leads his children on
to the place where he is gone.

Looking at these types of hymns now, you think, 'What kind of piety is that to give the children? How dare we encourage the children to believe that before they reach puberty they will be taken up to heaven to walk about in a white nightgown with Jesus Christ?' But for children who had been bereft of their siblings a hundred years ago, it was very important.

There are plenty of big issues today: ecology, child abuse, the verbal and physical maltreatment of women, the globalisation of technology and information, and the indebtedness with which the northern hemisphere has burdened the southern hemisphere. Where are the hymns that deal with these? Something has happened in our religious vocabulary, as well as in our religious imagination, which prohibits the kind of honesty of explanation which our Victorian forebears enjoyed. The people at the end of the twentieth century do not seem to be able to do this. I think this is partly to do with the form of the hymn and the anthem. The received form of Church music has impeded the linguistic and musical progress of God's people from being honest in the twentieth century. We are nice rather than honest. This is nothing to do with whether or not we should have guitars, loudspeakers and things like that. Again, we have not had many wordsmiths who are capable of reflecting the real experience of human beings or the reality of God in contemporary language and the reality of our relationship with God expressed by the writers of hymns and prayer.

Editors: It could be said, couldn't it, that a lot of the Church music, which provides the counter-culture to the traditional organ and choir, such as worship group and guitar band, sounds very 'American' in its sentimentality and piety?

Yes, it is sentimental, pious, escapist, and religious in a debilitating sense. It is not as secular as the psalms – they are the standard for Church praise. I think my feeling in the matter is that where hymnody and prayer reflect the genuine aspirations and agonies of people, it happens when the writer or writers are in constant dialogue with real people. There are maybe three things that they have to do: one, to be in constant dialogue with people, not with imagined people but with real people; two, to be in constant dialogue with God and with the scriptures; three, to differentiate between performance and participation.

There is a whole lot of contemporary worship songs, to my mind, in the same aura as anthems by Byrd and Tighe and Gibbons; in as much as they rely on professionals, or good amateurs, making a sound with voice and instruments, which only they can make. But it is not possible for everybody in the congregation to sing an anthem by Orlando Gibbons, or for everybody in the congregation to put a guitar round his or her neck and to make a contemporary worship song come alive. And the cameos of hymnody and prayer, which properly speak for the people, have to be participative. These can only be participative, if the writer articulates what people feel and what many people will be able to say or to sing together.

Now if you are schooled as many of us were, solely with regard to your religious formation, in assemblies where you study liturgy and all the rest of it, then the possibility of that happening is limited. A theological training, for most of us who are ordained, is a performance training. It is training to be a solo star in front of an audience on a Sunday morning. It is not, 'how can I enable these people to interact with the word of God'. When I ask people who are training for ministry, 'Do you ever get taught about enabling participative prayer? Do you ever get taught about lay models of leadership and worship? Do you ever get taught about how to do a Bible study or read the prayer book?' No, no. And the same is true of those who would want to be the writers of hymnody.

Because of my position in the Church of Scotland, every week people send me hymns which they believe the Holy Spirit has given to them the night before. I would give it back to the Holy Spirit, because I really do not believe that this is the kind of thing which speaks of anybody's experience apart from your own. There is a difference between a personal poem and a public hymn. I claim no excessive virtue or superiority in the writing of the people whom I represent, but one of the things which has been important to us, and we have learned this from our Celtic heritage, is that we would never dare publish, or offer to anybody else, either prayer or hymn, unless it had been run past the whole worship group of eighteen people. They would criticise, take it to bits, put it together again and maybe even discard it. If it is discarded, it would never see print. And then it will have been used over maybe two or three or four or five years, and only after that, after it had been honed and tested and its value affirmed, would we regard it as being something which speaks to or for the people and be offerable to anybody else.

So many people say, 'I've got a song. Can I get it published?' Or, 'I've just thought up these great prayers and I would like to offer them to the Church at large.' Fair enough, if you want to offer your personal meditations before the Lord with all humility and to make them public. But, if you are saying that these are songs of praise which all of God's people may enjoy, and yet you have never allowed people to say that they are awful, then I think you are on a hiding to nothing. You are not being participative, or communal, or allowing liturgy to be the work of the people. You are turning your offering into a performance art, where you hope people will goggle or be amazed at your innate or acquired abilities.

Editors: How would you set about liberating the Church, in the sort of way you describe, so that clergy, lay readers and lay preachers enable people to respond in worship, scripture and life, able to bring their own lives in to God's presence and go out into their own lives from the place of worship?

This is a major pedagogical question, if I can use a word which is more popular on the continent than in Britain. The answer may be found firstly in belief and, secondly, in technique.

Belief

One of my passions is to get a congregation to sing. I love it, and I love seeing it happen. I love seeing people transformed and I love hearing people say, 'I have never sung since I was fourteen and tonight I sang for the first time in thirty years.' That, for me, is a professional or a personal fulfilment. But I know that it is not a matter of technique. Essentially it is a matter of belief. If I believe that people will sing, then my bearing, and my approach to them, my anticipation, will liberate them to do that. If I believe that only choirs can sing, that only those who read music can sing, that only people who have an IQ of above 120 can sing, then my bearing, my belief and my language will limit the number who participate.

When we deal with evangelisation, engagement in prayer and with an appreciation of the Bible, there has to be a basic belief that people can do this. I do not know that this is something which the Church always engenders in its leadership. I think we train people for leadership who have a personal doctrine of substitutionary atonement. 'I will do the praying for everybody else. I will do the biblical reflection for everybody else.' Not, 'I will enable other people to pray or other people to reflect on scripture, because underneath I believe they can do it.'

With one of my colleagues I spent two years in a very poor parish in Glasgow where everyone had left school at the age of fourteen. We tried to discover ways in which people would be enabled to share the leadership of worship. The first thing we had to do was to discover how these people could talk about the Bible because they had never been enabled to do that before. I realised both that I had a mental block and that I did not think that this actually could happen. All my biblical reflection had been done with books at the seminary and it took a long while for me to discover that my approach to scripture and prayer was different from other people's. Once I began to believe that these folk, twelve of whom came every Thursday night for two years, had a capacity to reflect theologically, to pray, to engage with the scripture, once the belief came, then the next move was forward.

Technique

A lecture format is good for maybe 25 per cent of the population, if you like listening to a good speech. My grandfather was a communist miner who left school at the age of twelve. He loved public oratory. He was not a believer, but he admired people who could preach. He used to go, when he was twenty, to some kind of co-operative educational trust, where professors in botany or archaeology would come to Kilmarnock, the town where he lived, and give a lecture for an hour and a half on the latest discoveries. He would love that, because, at that time, the only pedagogical method was lecturing. The Church was the place where everyone was exposed to it. You had either expository sermons of forty-five minutes in some of the Free Churches or you had homilies which went on far too long. People were exposed to a form of communication which relied on the skills of an orator.

The twentieth century has completely changed that, not least because the medium of television is the predominant mode by which people receive communication. It becomes the standard by which other communications are engaged. If you have a dominant medium of television, where the image changes every 3.5 seconds, you never see the prime minister making a speech of fifteen minutes. He makes a speech of maybe a minute and a half and there are over twenty camera angles in the middle of it. The Church may offer a talking head and nothing more. Even a talking head with visual illustration, or overhead projection, is still about learning from one person, rather than learning by engagement with each other.

We had to learn to go back to an approach which echoed the Celtic era. Even with regard to the Bible, we used a whole lot of pictorial imagery. We began to get people to talk about and look at pictures, because these folk were unlettered. They never read books, but they could talk about pictures. We used to do very interesting Bible studies, where we would lay a whole series of cards and pictures of people and ask, 'who do you think is Mary Magdalene and why do you think it's her? Who do you think is Zaccheus and why do you think it's him?' The people began by using these visual stimuli to engage with the story. There is a need to enable people to say, not, 'What does this story mean?' (because that is the question of theological understanding, beloved of those with professional training), but, 'Who do I know who has been in this situation? Has there been a time in my life when I would have wanted to say this thing to God?'

Again, people will never entrust themselves to pray with each other or to relate their life to the life of God, unless they are within a community which is open and affirming. Once, in the Church of Scotland, I was given responsibility for a committee of the Church. At first, this committee met at a time which was inappropriate for lay people. So it was only ever clergy who attended. It was a committee that would spend endless hours wrangling about form and precedent and not about the substance of how you engage people in making music for the Church. When we met in the evening, it did not satisfy the traditionalists (the ministers wanted to meet in the morning, but the musicians could only make the evening). We had an evening meal for an hour before we ever talked; and it was the meal which enabled people to loosen up. We did not discuss business at the meal; we just talked about anything, and then people felt we were all on a common journey, that we are actually quite decent guys and that we can get on with each other. Only then would we get on with the business, meeting for maybe two and a half hours. We would do an immense quantity of highly creative work because we trusted each other.

I do not see within many Churches that kind of pre-evangelistic engagement. Most of us meet in churches for business, whether the business is parish council or Bible Study. People go to Bible Study in church and then come away from it. There may only ever be twelve people going to this Bible study. You seldom have forty or fifty. There are the faithful few who come who really exalt in the kind of status of being the faithful few.

Someone from a very charismatic congregation once described his house group as so dull. 'We come home from the office, get our dinner, rush out because it starts at 7.00pm, open with a prayer, then we open the Bible; we talk about what God's Word means; we close with coffee at 8.30pm, and somebody will go home because they want to have coffee with their wife or husband or friend; and we never actually talked about whether the Bible means anything in our present lives. Maybe, if we were to meet at 7.00pm, have coffee, and then do nothing but talk about the kind of day we have had or what is beggaring us; only then, maybe, when we open God's Word, will we bring ourselves to God's Word. We will not bring a caricature of the model Christian or the business man, who is still working on a business agenda'.

I recognise that the Alpha course begins with a meal together and it is a shame that it has taken us till the end of the twentieth century to discover a dynamic human activity of which Jesus was very fond. In Luke's Gospel, hardly a chapter goes past without Jesus talking about food, eating food with other people, inviting himself to dinner or inviting other people into a dinner where he is already the guest. But, although the Alpha course works on that principle to get people together, it then goes into the priestly model, where somebody takes charge and where free exploration is perhaps not as open as it could be. Of course, Alpha never sets itself out to be a regular congregational Bible study. It has a programme to go through.

I think we can take from it the fact that, when people are in community with each other, they are open to much more. I live next to the church in the caretaker's house and occasionally my colleague and I are asked to look in to see if the heating is on. So one night about five years ago we were asked to look in and make sure the heating was on in two rooms; one was the room where the finance committee of the church was going to meet, and the other was the room where women were meeting to plan a Holy Week Service. In the room where the finance committee were going to meet there were straight rows of seats all facing a table behind which the minister would sit (and behind him his predecessors looked down from photographs on the wall). The other room had been set up by the women. There were comfortable chairs, set in a circle; a candle was going to be lit in the middle. A coffee machine with fresh coffee was waiting to be percolated and there were scones that someone had baked that afternoon. I know which group I would rather go to. Consider: if the finance committee were to have that kind of model for meetings, they would still make decisions which were responsible, but finance would be something which was not set apart from faith, but part of faith.

As it happened, the women produced a very good liturgy for Holy Week. These are not the answers by any means. They give people a cup of tea and let them talk to each other. Then you may have a lively, vibrant church. But, in a society where the mode of communication is now dominated by televisual images that change every 3.5 seconds, this picture says something about how we have to question the way in which we communicate.

We live in a society where community is not a given any longer, as it was a given for the Celts and for the Benedictines. Community is a prerequisite for Anglican worship, whether willingly, because defined parish boundaries and common worship seemed right, or because parishes were formed under duress from the Lord of the manor (not the Lord in Heaven!). Even though the Lord of the manor commanded his serfs to be there, they still had a relationship with each other. We cannot presume this familiarity in parishes today, with city- or town-centre congregations, where people will bypass another three church doors to get to the one they want. Then they sit as strangers, relying on one person to do the liturgy for them and then disappear. When community is not a given in society, and if the Word of God has to percolate through the experience of people, then the Church has to enable real community, on both a small and large scale, to be a real experience for people, rather than a concept occasionally heard at prayers or sung about in hymns.

Editors: Would you say that the Church has withdrawn into its own culture and is unable to address the great issues of the world and society in the way that it might?

In some places the Church is drawn into its own culture. It is interesting that in South Africa, you have people like Tutu, very much an Anglican, very much an archbishop, but able to address the reality of his nation. It was clear with Oscar Romero in El Salvador, clear with Camera in northern Brazil, that there was engagement between them and society. They had an ability to speak both within the Church about that which belonged to the Church, and in the world about that with belonged to the world.

If you believe that the World is Caesar's and that the Church is God's, then you are never able to address the world. If you believe that God so loved, not the Church, not even humanity, but the world; that he sent his Son to redeem the world, then your vocabulary, imagery and imagination has always to be informed by the things of the world. I think that sometimes, when officials of the Church speak about political or social events, they sounds naïve, with a desire for simplistic solutions. The thing about

Romero and Tutu is that they lived in the middle of a turmoil which physically impinged on their lives and they could not be neutral about it.

I think that, if we cocoon ourselves in religious environment and religious language, then, when we begin to speak about that which affects other people, it sounds naïve. It may also be the case that one of the objectives of the Church in the new millennium should not be that we have more bishops or priests who are versed in the matter of international debt or of family issues or any other issue of social momentum. We should have the lay people who are engaged with these issues all the time, and who also have sufficient biblical and theological understanding, to represent the Church to the world. Why are confirmed Christians with relevant professional knowledge not asked to speak on these matters? We have Christians in medicine, engaged in the issues of life and death, and ethics and biological engineering. Why do we have to wait until some bishop has read the appropriate paper before he makes a speech? Why do we not say, 'Here is a lay person, whom God has called in the vocation of medicine; he or she will make this statement with the encouragement of the Church.'

We do not do this, because too often they are biblically and theologically naïve. What we do not see is that the bishop can be as naïve, socially or medically, in the eyes of the general public. It would be greatly to the Church's advantage, if on issues of social, political and economic importance, we were to enable the professionals to comment theologically on the Church's behalf. (This would be better than hoping the bishop will get it right when he speaks on a matter outside his normal expertise.)

Editors: Would you like to say something more about the relationship between worship and action in the context of 'Christian community', that is, through engagement in the issues of the world, and discovering worship that enables you to do this?

This may sound a bit naïve, but I believe that what we sing determines what we believe. So that is why many people in Britain have a limited christology. They know that, when Jesus was born in a stable, he never cried, and that he was a model child. The next minute he died on a cross with his arms outspread. What he did in the thirty-three years in between is a mystery because we have precious few hymns and songs that deal with the message of Christ. Therefore, we do not engage ourselves in a world of action, partly because we do not sing that is what Christ did in his public ministry. Perhaps it is only when we begin to pray about the prickly realities of life, and begin to offer our praise to God arising from our experience, that we may feel impelled or propelled into dealing with them.

At present, with the Jubilee 2000 Millennium petition to cancel Developing World debt, Church people are being encouraged to write to their governments. This has caused me to realise that, with the exception of the Scottish version of the Lord's Prayer, which says, 'forgive us our debts', 'debt' is not a word that crops up in any hymn or prayer anywhere. This is an economic reality of life for a sizable proportion of humanity, but we do not have any hymns or songs that deal with economic imperialism or with people who have to work with a burden of debt or struggle with a low income. My belief is that, because we don't have that language in our prayer or song, people see this as being peripheral to Christian witness. Material, which my colleagues and I have written, has been composed because, either we have had to engage with folk for whom this is a reality, or, because we realised that it is just not there in the Church's vocabulary.

Somebody has to produce relevant songs for world and personal debt. The interesting thing is that, when people have been enabled in terms of scripture, prayer and song to see that this is not something divorced from faith, but a biblical injunction (see Leviticus, Psalms and Isaiah in Luke's Gospel), then their willingness to engage both politically and experientially is fuelled. I think there are occasions when, if within the life of our local community or a

National Church there are particular social issues which cry out for the pain being flung at heaven, it has to be flung and a word from God sought. We should be encouraging the productions of writing and the discovery of materials which allow for the articulation of that particular subject, in order that people can feel that it is tied up with real faith rather than being peripheral to it.

For example, the Orkney child abuse case years ago was something which was big in public debate and I remember a church in Scotland asking if my colleagues and I would go and do some worship on a topical issue. So I said, 'Well this child abuse thing is topical, but where would you look for any resources to deal with that?' We ended up with the story of Solomon, with the two women disputing over who was the mother of a child. Solomon said, 'Okay, cut it in two and you can have half each.' At that time it was a very appropriate biblical story to use, because, within the child abuse case, you had the social workers saying the child should be ours, the parents saying the child should be theirs, police saying the child went into care or custody... and in the middle of this the child was pulled apart. Who was looking after the holistic welfare of that child? Because that was what the story from the Old Testament addresses. I am really glad that we were forced to go for it. But how do you symbolically offer the confusion or the pain of people who have been affected by child abuse? I remember vividly that service of worship because it was not like any other. People left the church in tears, people walked out in the middle of it; partly because some of these people had been the victims of abuse and had never felt that their pain would be represented in the public worship of almighty God.

And I wonder what other areas of life there are where people's experience, which should have been offered to God, has been precluded because our worship has either depended on expository preaching, which would never touch these issues, or where the vocabulary of hymn and prayer has never been as vivid as the Psalms in offering deep agony. I think, for some people, help does not come unless they are able to curse, and to name that which has been vindictive to them, and to shout to heaven to say, 'Where the hell God are you in the middle of this atrocious mess?' It is not very polite language, but if people in the Old Testament could do that, and if Jesus had on his lips every word of the psalms, as indeed blessed St Cuthbert did, then why do we always have to be polite? God calls us to be real, to be honest, not to be nice. This is for me the basis of faith, a real encounter between the raw experience of my life and the raw experience of Jesus Christ. It is not role-play, and whenever it becomes role-play, direct engagement is prohibited.

Editors: *One of the problems between relating worship to action seems that the exercise often is limited to smallish groups, action groups, people who are particularly concerned. Now you have opened up for us the possibility that song and hymn may be able to engage the whole Church in a much wider, more corporate way.*

Yes, if we believe it is the Body of Christ and that we are not all kidney, all liver, all hand and all the rest of it. I do not expect that everybody in the congregation will be carrying the torch for feminism or that anybody in the congregation will be carrying a torch for the Multiple Sclerosis Society or that everybody in the congregation will be passionately involved in the Free Angola from Land Mines Committee, but I do believe that part of my responsibility, as being a member of the Body of Christ, is to hold, sometimes in love and sometimes in tension, those who have felt that their faith impels them to be concerned with this, that and the next thing. I would want the prayer and the song of the Church to reflect where they are and to encourage them and I would want them to have my empathy. I cannot always guarantee them my wholehearted engagement.

I would want there to be, in any Church of which I was a member, people who were passionate conservatives and people who were passionate socialists and I would want to be able to argue with those who were of an opposing political opinion. Heaven cannot wait for us all to get the right opinion or angle on any number of the major political and social dilemmas that face the world at the present time. Heaven's not going to wait until we are all signed up to the correct party. Within the Church I think that we can fairly allow for the diversity of our pastoral locations to be reflected in prayer and song, and if that for some people opens up an avenue of existential engagement, we are going well. Unless it is there in the prayer and the song of the Church, people will feel it is no concern of ours and we have a very cosy Christianity which is just to do with my soul, my death, and my children's baptism.

Editors: Would you say there is any future in the new millennium for the cosy Church or the introverted Church or will there be a Church surviving very far into the next millennium?

Well, that is really God's worry. I am not really an ecclesiologist. I am fascinated by the Church, its foibles, ancestry and all the rest of it, but I am not into introducing or thinking of a master plan for our continued existence. I believe that God will use the Church in the form it exists for as long as it is required. If that form has to be transformed or changed beyond present recognition, then that need not be seen as an indication of failure on the part of the Church of the twentieth century. Rather, it may be indicative of God's delight in transformation and resurrection. If we believe that Jesus Christ rose from the dead and if we engage with a God who has made the divine well known in the scriptures, then we cannot expect ever that we or our Church shall remain the same. There is no biblical evidence from Genesis to Revelation that anyone who has come into contact with the living God remains the same. This is not to say that every change is good. It is not to say that we should be in constant flux, just that the central dynamic of Christian existence involves change. A big question for Jesus is whether he will remain an inert corpse or come back to life. If that is the dynamic which is at the centre of Christ's life and our traditional faith, then we have to expect to be in the process of transformation.

And we sing great hymns when we sing, 'changed from glory into glory'. But, if we are praying to God that we will be changed from glory into glory, this might be in the sense that we are going to burn all the pews and make a fresh start. We cannot move the one thing and then forbid the reality to happen in our experience. If I had a magic wand, among other things with which I would want to endow the Church, is a positively healthy and biblical understanding that change is not the enemy of faith, but the central dynamic. Jesus did not go up to people who were lepers and say he was sorry for them and that he hoped they would be still there when he came back in two weeks' time, so that he could give them a lollipop. All those who encountered him, even the Pharisees who loathed him, were affected for good, or in their case sometimes for evil, by his word and his presence. If the Church is the Body of Christ, and we exhibit no sign of transformation, we are the corpse of Christ, not the Corpus Christi. It is as plain as that.

The only other thing that I would add is that I am hopeful, not optimistic, because I think optimism is a shallow thing and hope is deep. I am hopeful for the Church in the next era, partly because I think, in distinction from the cynicism of my teens and my twenties (a cynicism which was there in great abundance and lavished on any congregation who had the misfortune to be afflicted by it), and, not because I'm in my middle years, but because I have identified places where, despite themselves, congregations are moving. I feel really hopeful. I think that the fabric, the physical fabric of the Church in many places will crumble and that the way in which we meet and the spells in which we worship will be transformed or changed. I think that will happen.

Sometimes a congregation of old people may bring us hope, not the inertia of nostalgia. We have a new ecumenical hymn book in

Scotland, 150 hymns. This old people's congregation in six months have learned 75 out of 150 new hymns and were singing them with gusto. I think of another congregation of old people where the way in which leadership of prayer, reading scripture, engagement with the Bible and the willingness to reflect publicly, has happened in the past few years. Among the very people whom previously their ministers or their leaders would say that we cannot do anything new because it will upset the old people, new things are happening.

Scripturally, it is the old people who are midwives of change. God calls Abraham and Sarah when they are in their retirement years to be those who will pioneer the future. God calls Zachariah and Elizabeth to be the ones with whom the nativity story begins and they are past child-bearing years. God calls Simeon and Hannah to be the ones who see this as a new thing which is happening and God is behind it. When we believe that old people are the midwives of the new order, and when we give them in our Church that status, rather than compel them to be introspective and backward-looking traditionalists, transformation takes place. Very often the powerful clergy are the voice of caution, but it is usually the old people who are conveniently blamed.

Liberated older people have a significant biblical presence. Hannah, in the story of Candlemas, is the one who sees Christ as the liberator of the people. What a role to give those whom people give up on! And you know, when I see congregations of elderly people beginning to take on new life and thereby being attractive for younger people, that gives me some hope, because often people just pastorally minister to the elderly or an ageing congregation, with no sense of expectation. So we exist in a kind of 1930s period, trying to recapture the youth of these people who are now in their seventies. It is totally unattractive to anybody else coming in because no one is able to live in a theme park of 1930's religion. When younger people see that in this group of older folk there is a dynamism, an openness, a life, an expectation, a welcome, an evident progress, they discover a more alluring congregation and community in which to be a part. The Church has to decide, 'Are we going to be a theme park, keeping to that culture which once was, or are we going to be a sign of transformation?' Where transformation happens, there is deep hope. Where we have a theme park mentality, there is deep distress. But I believe there is hope.

HEAVEN SHALL NOT WAIT

Heaven shall not wait
For the poor to lose their patience,
The scorned to smile, the despised to find a friend:
Jesus is Lord;
He has championed the unwanted;
In him injustice confronts its timely end.

Heaven shall not wait
For the rich to share their fortunes,
The proud to fall, the elite to tend the least:
Jesus is Lord;
He has shown the master's privilege –
To kneel and wash servants' feet before they feast.

Heaven shall not wait
For the dawn of great ideas,
Thoughts of compassion divorced from cries of pain:
Jesus is Lord;
He has married word and action;
His cross and company make his purpose plain.

Heaven shall not wait
For our legalised obedience,
Defined by statute, to strict conventions bound:
Jesus is Lord;
He has hallmarked true allegiance –
Goodness appears where his grace is sought and found.

Heaven shall not wait
For triumphant Hallelujahs,
When earth has passed and we reach another shore:
Jesus is Lord
In our present imperfection;
His power and love are for now and then for evermore.

Wild Goose Songs, vol. 1,
John Bell and Graham Maule (1987)

A PRAYER OF THE VENERABLE BEDE

I implore you good Jesus
that as in your mercy
you have given me to drink in with delight
the words of your knowledge,
so of your loving kindness
you will also grant me one day to come to you,
the fountain of all wisdom,
and to stand for ever before your face.
Amen.

EPILOGUE

WEAVING THE THEMES TOGETHER

Linda Burton and *Alex Whitehead*

Throughout the book, our contributors have sought to revisit the spiritual roots of British Christianity, seeing how the broad streams of Celtic and Benedictine spirituality flow together for our great blessing and in joyful response to the God we worship and serve. We have been conscious of the turning of the millennium, not with the sense of mystery, awe and dread sometimes experienced by the curiously religious seeking for portents (after all, we asked David Jenkins to deal with the Book of Revelation), but with a sense of attraction to further pilgrimage and exploration by the one whom Revelation describes as the Alpha and Omega, the beginning and end of all time and all endeavour.

Our contributors are all people who have lived, and are living in the present, looking to the future with a critical but hopeful perspective, sharing between them a very wide-ranging vision and helping us to focus on the streams of faith which continue to inspire them.

Emerging from the chapters, prayers and hymns is a desire to involve all God's people in the *missio Dei*, the calling and sending of ordinary (but becoming extraordinary) folk, by the dynamic God, who brings Unity to the activity of Trinity. Memories of a Conference, designed to help a particularly Anglican form of Lay Ministry (that of Licensed Reader), have turned into an aspiration for all God's laity. There is a desire to discover, value and encourage the enormous and often neglected potential of active, half-recognised and latent vocation to be worked out in every part and member of the Body of Christ. Only minds open to being illuminated by a light which comes from both the deepest places and broadest horizons, will find the perception to embrace and celebrate such a wholehearted sense of vocation.

This has obvious implications for formal structures of ministry, where partnership and collaboration between ordained and lay ministers will be the norm for all ministry. Yet current and, inevitably, future problems created by a shortage of ordained ministry, will not disappear by evoking and training an increasing number of lay ministers to enlarge ministerial teams or more than compensate for the decline in paid clergy.

A task for both lay and ordained ministers will be that of supporting, enabling and encouraging all Christians to explore their vocation and become the authentic voice of the Church at workplace, play, in public life and domestically.

Lois Green warns of simply turning lay ministers into the role formerly performed more exclusively by the clergy.

> There are intricate hierarchies, both in the professional structures of the Church of England, and in the committee structures of Non-conformity: terms such as 'Steward', 'Elder', 'Pastor', 'Class Leader', 'Superintendent', all emphasise a control model.[1]

We could add 'Reader' and simply try to move the problem along, without addressing the real need for change and transformation. Lois Green continues:

> The way through these problems may be very difficult to find, but it has to do with enabling and empowering. It means the clergy enabling the laity to articulate their concerns... and the laity developing for themselves an appropriate and holistic role in public life and requesting the clergy to help equip them for it.[2]

We would like to propose that the best way of enabling and empowering is to let in the light of 'Christ the Morning Star'. 'Empowering' then becomes an appeal to the guiding and inspiring power of the Spirit ever bringing Christ into true focus in our perceptions. Professor Dan Hardy, in an unpublished talk to the clergy of Stockton-on-Tees in 1991, described the work of the priest (and we would like to extend this possibility to the appointed lay minister) as a 'ministry of understanding', that is, 'standing under' the Church to enable it to fulfil its vocation. This is a serving and supporting ministry, assuming that the visible and outward-moving profile of the Church will be seen through the activity of its lay members. By presiding at the sacraments or drawing the people together in worship, prayer, preaching and teaching, ordained and lay ministers will help the Church to understand who it is and what it is. The 'understanding' ministry will never be deluded into thinking it is the Church or the most important visible part of it.

Just as, throughout this book, we have endeavoured to revisit our spiritual roots, as a way of finding inspiration for the way ahead, we may now turn to some very old biblical models to find refreshingly contemporary clues and examples. They present themselves as Promise, Covenant and Community.

Right back in the beginning, well, as far back as Abraham (and that is far enough for now), we find God calling Abraham to journey in faith with, at least in part, the altruistic purpose of bringing blessings on all the nations of the world. To enable this to happen, his descendants will become as numerous as the grains of sand on the seashore and called to be a Chosen People, moving onwards and outwards to help fulfil God's reconciling and healing mission for the world. This is a People of Promise, receiving promises from God and being called to be the fulfiller of promises for the world.

Further along what turned out to be a none-too-comfortable journey, God invites them to be a Covenant People, bound to God in a Covenant relationship defined in terms of Law ('Law' in which the Psalmist claims to 'delight'. Psalm 119).

The People of Promise, called to bring blessings on the nations, are to be a Holy People in a Covenant relationship with God. This relationship was not only offered to the prophet/priest/leader/judge,

Moses, or to Aaron and the secondary leadership, but to all the people, who were equally in Covenant with God and each other. Their leadership, even when we think of such great leaders as Moses and Samuel, was to be an enabling leadership, in order that the Holy People would understand, accept and cheerfully respond to their vocation.

This story is so familiar that we may completely miss its revolutionary implications. In the story of the mature Samuel we may easily dismiss him as being a cantankerous old man, jealous of his own waning status among the Tribes. He argues powerfully against the nation's request for a king, in order for them to be like the other nations. But they were not to become like the other nations, they were to be uniquely God's chosen people, an example, sign and blessing to the other nations. If they became like the others, what would become of their vocation and in what way would all the people share in God's calling, Promise and Covenant? The coming of the kings would introduce hierarchy, an unnecessary class system and ultimately the suppression and diminution of most of the people, who would forget that the vocation chiefly involved all of them. The cutting edge of their call would be blunted.

God's vocation is for the whole people. This Old Testament insight, going back over three millennia, is a judgement and challenge for the Church of the third Christian millennium.

This thread of insight is woven throughout the 'Church thinking' of St Paul. Over and over again he rises above the limitations, prejudices and practices of a 'Pharisee of Pharisees' to find that vocation contains that which is universal and egalitarian. Salvation is also for the Gentiles, and so Paul must be an Apostle to the Gentiles. He recognises the need for specialised ministry, and that there will be leadership roles. He sometimes needs to assert that he is an Apostle and embrace the suffering and accountability that seems to go with true apostolic ministry. In the Christian Church the Apostle is one who serves, who is beaten and shipwrecked, 'For we do not proclaim ourselves; we proclaim Jesus Christ as Lord and ourselves as your slaves for Jesus' sake' (2

Corinthians 3:5). Here Paul is echoing the words of Jesus who surprised his disciples by depicting that the 'Son of Man came not to be served, but to serve, and to give his life a ransom for many' (Mark 10:4-5). Is this too revolutionary for today's Church?

While recognising the value of some leadership roles and the cost of being an Apostle, Paul constantly asserts that all the baptised share God's gifts and are equally precious, valued and redeemed in the sight of God. All are made brothers and sisters of Jesus by adoption and children of God (see Galatians 4:6, 7).

The gifting of this New Testament view of the Church, seen through Paul's eyes, is to recognise that God's gifts are dispersed throughout the whole Community. There is an expectation that all the baptised have received gifts from God and that these gifts are to be shared by the whole Church as it moves outward into the world. The famous 'Body' imagery in 1 Corinthians 12 reminds us that 'those members of the body that we think less honourable we clothe with greater honour, and our less respectable members are treated with greater respect... the members may have the same care for one another. If one member suffers, all suffer together with it; if one member is honoured, all rejoice together with it' (1 Corinthians 12: 23-26).

The Church of the new millennium will be continuous with the Church now. No doubt there will continue to be Readers and even priests and bishops. But the driving, outward-looking force of the millennium ministry will be a laity who recognise their sense of vocation and their relationship with and mutual support for each other. This will be a laity who will not be 'ashamed to confess the faith of Christ crucified' and to be faithful 'soldiers and servants' in the world.

To advance this exciting prospect for the Church and the world, Christians must optimistically revisit their spiritual roots for wisdom and depth; shallow plants die in the heat of the day. Surely, for the Church in England, it would be a great blessing for Celtic Spirituality to meet Benedictine Rule, for Christ the Morning Star to rise in the psychology of ordinary Christians, who, rooted in Bible, prayer, and the Community of sacrament, silence and song, will embrace the new millennium with a living faith and a bright hope.

NOTES

1. Lois Green, 'The Two Cultures', in *Changing World, Unchanging Church*, David Clarke (ed.), (Mowbray, 1997).
2. ibid., p. 67.
3. ibid., p. 68.
All biblical quotations in this chapter are from *The New Revised Standard Edition*.

SISTERS AND BROTHERS

Sisters and brothers, with one voice
Confirm your calling and rejoice;
Each is God's child and each God's choice.
Alleluia! Alleluia! Alleluia!

Strangers no more, but cherished friends,
Live as the body God intends,
Sharing the love the Spirit sends
Alleluia! Alleluia! Alleluia!

Not, though, by wisdom, wealth or skill,
Nor by ourselves can we fulfil
What, for the world, is God's own will.
Alleluia! Alleluia! Alleluia!

Christ is the way. By him alone,
Seeds of the kingdom's life are sown,
Patterns of heaven on earth are shown.
Alleluia! Alleluia! Alleluia!

Then follow him through every day.
Fear not what crowds or critics say:
Those on the move stir those who stay.
Alleluia! Alleluia! Alleluia!

In factory, office, home or hall.
Where people struggle, strive or stall,
Seek out and serve the Lord of All.
Alleluia! Alleluia! Alleluia!

Seeking and serving, with one voice
Confirm your calling and rejoice:
Each is God's child and each God's choice.
Alleluia! Alleluia! Alleluia!

WGRG,
Iona Community, Glasgow (1995)

CONTRIBUTORS

Esther de Waal, lecturer and author of books on Celtic and Benedictine Spirituality

David Day, Principal of St John's College, Durham, lecturer and author in both education and preaching, a Reader in the Church of England

Angela Ashwin, lecturer, retreat conductor and author of books on prayer and spirituality

David Jenkins, formerly Bishop of Durham, lecturer and author

Christopher Mayfield, Bishop of Manchester and Chairman of the Central Readers' Council

John Bell, a minister of the Church of Scotland, musician, composer and a founder of the Wild Goose Resource Group

Alison White, an Anglican Priest, Durham Diocesan Director of Ordinands and formerly Director of Mission and Pastoral Studies, St John's College, Durham

Clare Lockhart, a Sister of Charity and priest in charge of Castletown, Sunderland

Kate Tristram, of Marygate House, Holy Island, formerly lecturer at the College of St Hild and St Bede, Durham University, and Honorary Canon of Newcastle

Robert Cooper, priest in charge of Sadberge and a Director of the Arts and Recreation Chaplaincy in the North East

Alan Smithson, Bishop of Jarrow and Chairman of the Durham Readers' Council

Linda Burton, Lecturer in Religious Education at Durham University, a Reader and Assistant Warden of Readers in the Durham Diocese

Alex Whitehead, vicar of St Peter's Stockton-on-Tees, Warden of Readers in the Durham Diocese and an Honorary Canon of Durham.